DATA ANALYSIS AND HARMONIZATION

JEFF VOIVODA

iUNIVERSE, INC.
BLOOMINGTON

Data Analysis and Harmonization

The views expressed in this work are solely those of the author and do not necessarily reflect the views of the publisher, and the publisher hereby disclaims any responsibility for them.

iUniverse books may be ordered through booksellers or by contacting:

iUniverse
1663 Liberty Drive
Bloomington, IN 47403
www.iuniverse.com
1-800-Authors (1-800-288-4677)

Because of the dynamic nature of the Internet, any web addresses or links contained in this book may have changed since publication and may no longer be valid.

Any people depicted in stock imagery provided by Thinkstock are models, and such images are being used for illustrative purposes only.

Certain stock imagery © Thinkstock.

ISBN: 978-1-4502-9824-7 (sc)
ISBN: 978-1-4502-9826-1 (dj)
ISBN: 978-1-4502-9825-4 (ebk)

Printed in the United States of America

iUniverse rev. date: 3/18/2011

ACKNOWLEDGEMENTS

First and foremost, I would like to thank my family for their continuous and unending support.

I would also like to thank Kathy Sowell. Kathy is the President of Custom Enterprise Solutions/SowellEAC and widely considered an expert in the field of Enterprise Architecture. She graciously provided a foreword for this book. Her unremitting dedication to the practices of Enterprise Architecture provides a wonderful example of just how pervasive the data disciplines have become.

In addition, I would like to thank Michael Drake. Mike is one of the top graphic artists in the industry and owner of the company Monkeebox, Inc. The illustrations he provided help drive home some of the critical points in this book by providing visual reminders of the ideas expressed in the text.

Finally, I would like to thank all the people who will read this book and utilize some or all of the ideas and concepts expressed within.

CONTENTS

Foreword

Enterprise Architecture and the Data Disciplines: A Symbiotic Relationship

by Kathy Sowell

When Jeff asked me to write a foreword to his book, I started thinking about the issues that are swirling in the enterprise architecture and data worlds today. Many of these issues involve the relationship between data and enterprise architecture. For example: Should an enterprise architecture contain a separate data view? Do we really need enterprise architecture as long as we have data modeling and data management? What is data without enterprise architecture? What is enterprise architecture without data? What is enterprise architecture, anyway? Is there really even any such thing as enterprise architecture?

Enterprise architecture is a relatively young discipline (although for those of us who have been in the trenches from the beginning, thirty years or so seems like a long time!). So I will not try to definitively answer these questions yet. The point I want to make now is only that enterprise architecture has a symbiotic relationship with the group of data-related disciplines that require analysis of data—data management, data and information quality, data architecture—and that, like all symbiotic relationships, this one can benefit all parties involved.

THE DATA DISCIPLINES AND ENTERPRISE ARCHITECTURE CAN BENEFIT EACH OTHER

The data disciplines have sometimes been seen as highly specialized exercises in manipulating zeros and ones, number crunching, or other tasks that normal people don't understand and don't want to understand. Enterprise architecture, on the other hand, has been criticized on many fronts: some see it as a high-level, touchy-feely management exercise conducted at the arm-waving level, others as an excruciatingly detailed IT exercise (see above), and others as a plain old fraud. When the two disciplines work together in an intelligent way, however, the data disciplines can provide real-world practicality to enterprise architecture, and enterprise architecture can add accessibility and an appropriate level of detail for decision making to the data disciplines. Let's look a little more closely at these benefits.

ENTERPRISE ARCHITECTURE PUTS DATA INTO CONTEXT

Enterprise architecture has a unique ability to exploit the potential of data analysis. How? By coaxing data out of the data stovepipe and enfolding it into a multifaceted, holistic study of a complete enterprise. Enterprise architecture has the ability to put data into context, making data analysis more meaningful and more fruitful. More specifically, enterprise architecture has the ability to:

1. represent different aspects of data in different, but logically consistent, artifacts that show how data operates in the enterprise; and

2. represent the different data requirements that arise in the different circumstances under which the enterprise must operate.

For example, an activity model shows data at an abstract level, that is, data that is exchanged between abstract activities. A business node connection model then translates this abstraction into the actual data that is exchanged between the physical business nodes that perform the abstract activities.

Under different scenarios, different data and information will be exchanged; a series of scenario sequence diagrams captures these different exchanges. And, in the different scenarios, the data requirements such as reliability, speed, accuracy, classification, and so on will be different; a corresponding series of information exchange matrices captures these differing requirements.

IT'S THE DATA, STUPID ... OR IS IT?: "HUMAN" DOES NOT MEAN "STUPID"

In addition to putting data into a meaningful context, *enterprise architecture has the ability to represent data in human-friendly forms, making it more accessible to decision makers and clarifying its message.* (The medium is still the message, even forty years after Marshall McLuhan made that point.)

It seems obvious that this human-friendly quality of data is necessary and desirable in order for decision makers to make good decisions. In fact, one of the main reasons behind the creation of enterprise architecture, at least in my experience, was to make data itself, the representation of data, and the analysis of data more accessible to (human) decision makers.

Lately, however, in some quarters of the enterprise architecture community, the meaning of the old saying "It's the data, stupid" has been twisted. Instead of being a somewhat primitive way of saying that data is very important, it has come to mean instead that data, like winning, isn't the most important thing, it is the only thing. More specifically, it has been used to imply that the representation of the data in ways that humans can understand, that is, through visual artifacts (pictures), is a dumbing down of the data and not worthy of grown-ups' effort. I believe this attitude is a mistake and prevents us from taking advantage of one of the most advantageous features of the symbiosis between data and enterprise architecture.

WHAT ABOUT THE FUTURE?: BUZZWORDS COME AND GO, BUT DATA LASTS FOREVER

Humans have been capturing and analyzing data for thousands of years, and we will continue to do so—we can't help ourselves. On the other hand, enterprise architecture, as a discipline of sorts, has been around for only twenty-five or thirty years, depending on how you define its birth. Even at that, people have been predicting its imminent demise for at least ten of those years.

Will enterprise architecture survive as a recognizable field of endeavor? Who knows? But in any case, the aspects of enterprise architecture that we have been addressing here—its ability to provide a context for the study of data and its ability to put a human face on data—will survive if we continue to provide for their care and feeding. We need to make sure that, whether the discipline of enterprise architecture survives and no matter how it evolves, we continue to take advantage of these aspects of enterprise architecture to enrich our conduct of the data disciplines.

INTRODUCTION

In my twenty-plus years of information technology consulting, I have been tossed into some pretty hectic situations. Whether it was to come in at project inception and get analysis activities off the ground, jump in midstream and get the data team over the proverbial hump, or worst of all hop directly into the frying pan after being directed to "save our bacon," I always found myself answering the same question: Where do we start?

This question is more than fair. In today's sophisticated business technology environment, the sheer volume of data that an entity ingests, processes, and disseminates to the rest of us is staggering. It really doesn't matter what industry, the amount of data being processed is enormous. If an analyst or a team of analysts is just getting the data analysis effort started, it can be quite overwhelming. If you start by identifying all the data an organization uses in its everyday operations and business processes, you can quickly come up with a multitude of files, databases, forms, interfaces, portals, spreadsheets, data marts, reference tables, and checklists that an organization uses to maintain the flow of data.

So, where do you start? The answer is simple: start at the beginning, man! Even when the amount of data for review and analysis has been enormous, I've always started by asking some pointed, straightforward questions. Where does this data come from? How does it get to where it's going? Who is at the other end to receive it? And who the heck cares about this data anyway? When I find the answers to these types of high-level questions, I quickly find myself moving in the right direction and, more important, lifting the data analysis effort off the ground and into flight!

Would you agree with the following statement? You can't accomplish much without knowing the facts. Oh, sure, you could fabricate a few things, maybe stretch the truth a bit here and there or embellish the details, but without some solid, accurate data, you really can't achieve your goals. At times, it can be difficult to obtain all the facts needed to make the correct decision—whether you are a defensive coordinator for an NFL team gathering the weaknesses of an opposing team and trying to stop a potent offensive charge or a surgeon preparing for an operation by collecting information on the vital signs and allergies of the patient or an automobile mechanic hooking a car engine up to a computer to gather diagnostics to figure out why the car won't start anymore. Regardless of the situation, a person, team, or organization gathers the relevant data before making a decision and taking action. This paradigm is especially true in the information technology (IT) field.

Collecting the data you need requires that the data is readily accessible and available. Harmonizing the data ensures that that can happen. Data harmonization is a process—a set of actions or operations—applied to a collection of raw, disparate data and resulting in a consistent set of standard, agreed-upon, comprehensive data elements that can be utilized and transmitted across, and between, the involved organizations.

Let's look more closely at some of the key words and phrases that comprise the definition. First, data harmonization is a process; in fact, it is an iterative process that will be applied many times before the desired end state is achieved. This process is applied to raw data (at least initially). As you will read in this book, at the beginning of the process, you will be faced with a rather large and unwieldy set of data elements of differing importance and utility. That's okay! At the early stage of harmonization, the more the merrier! Last, the resulting data set should be standardized, agreed upon, and comprehensive. Remember, the objective of data harmonization—and your goal as a data analyst—is to provide a comprehensive set of data that can be easily understood, communicated, and fully utilized by your clients.

For many years, I worked for a major petroleum company that was a global competitor in the crude oil market. The company processed an enormous amount of data on a daily basis. It collected data on movement of product through the pipelines, volumes being stored in tanks across the country (so-called tank farms), gallons of product being transported by tanker trunks on American roadways, and even how much petroleum was sold at individual stations. One of the main reasons this company was so successful was all the data that pertained to the products was standardized across all the divisions and departments. When the marketing department sent data to the supply organization, the product was described in exactly the same manner on both sides of the transaction. There was no need to convert the data, no need for translation routines, and no time lost for decision makers who could not get their hands on the right data at the right time. These are only some of the wonderful benefits of data harmonization. There are plenty more!

In this book, we'll talk about the process of gathering the much-needed data that we seek. I've written this book from the following point of view: You and I have been hired by a client to analyze and consolidate their disparate data stores. As you'll quickly find out, their data is redundantly held, poorly formatted, and inadequately maintained. But don't worry—we're going to fix it together! We'll start by identifying our sources of data. We'll discuss the problems and anomalies that could (and most likely will) arise when an organization's data is managed inefficiently, ineffectively, and disparately. Once all the data sources have been gathered and analyzed, we'll discuss the process of harmonization: where to begin, how to progress, and how to achieve your ultimate goal of a standardized harmonized data set (HDS).

I will also take some time to discuss the advantageous features of various tools that are available to assist you in your analysis and presentations, as well as offer advice on presenting, discussing, and garnering feedback on your artifacts and work products with the client. I'll include some discussion of determining business processes and defining how they relate to data collection and harmonization. I'll spend some time reviewing a handful of the organizations and governing bodies that enforce industry-wide data standards that you may need to be aware of and conform to. Additionally, I'll talk about potential next steps in the analysis cycle and offer guidance on how all this hard data harmonization work can be leveraged, exploited, and put to good use. All the while, we'll be helping an import business to identify and harmonize their data assets using the methods I describe in the following chapters. You will be able to see how effective the process can be and how easy it will be to successfully produce data artifacts. Always keep this in mind: corporate data is a corporate asset—manage it!

CHAPTER 1

THIS ORGANIZATION
HAS PROBLEMS

Let's suppose for a minute that you are the person responsible for producing and disseminating a voluminous (and dreaded) "monthly" report. By good luck or bad, by knowledge or naivety, you're the poor sap who has to locate, collect, manipulate, crunch, grind, produce, and distribute this information to coworkers, colleagues, stakeholders, and clients.

First things first, let's gather all the required data. Okay, gathering all the required data isn't as easy as it sounds. As a top-notch employee, you know that sales figures come from the sales system. That's housed in the sales department. You also know the inventory totals are stored over in the warehouse system, part of the inventory management department. You can't access that system, but you can get Bob to dump those numbers into a file so you can use them (hopefully, Bob isn't

1

on vacation!). Oh yes, and the expired customers need to be notified that their accounts are about to be closed. Who do you call for that, again? Oh, right, customer service has that data. You better get cracking!

Once you receive the sales figures, don't forget to apply the conversion program because sales volumes are expressed in pieces and the inventory amounts are expressed in components. Also, the part number associated with the pieces in the sales system can contain alphabetic characters, but the part number used for components in the warehouse system is only numeric. And you can't forget to review the product descriptions since the sales system truncates the description field at twenty-five characters, so the forty character description fields from inventory system sometimes just don't make sense. If there are any problems, you'll have to print out the inconsistencies and make certain the report lists both part numbers from both systems and send it to Jane in the quality control (QC) department for her to review and (hopefully) rectify the problems. Of course, all this needs to be completed before the final report is delivered. While that's transpiring, you better start reviewing the list of expired accounts. Last month, we sent four expiration notices to the same person because the addresses were basically the same, except for some slight differences in each record in the database. How embarrassing!

DOES THIS PROBLEM SOUND FAMILIAR?

Should we continue this confusing, ineffective scenario, or do you get the picture? I think we can easily see this process needs some streamlining, and with little trouble we can spot the inefficiencies. Although, the poor processing and data issues were exaggerated to make the point, there are indeed some organizations that operate in a haphazard way that is alarmingly similar to this disjointed and ineffective manner described in the scenario. Maybe you've even been part of a mess like this! I know I have!

A few years ago, I was working with a government agency that processed applications and issued certifications to applicants based on the data contained in the applications. There were two basic requirements to get the agency-issued certification: First, the application had to be complete, which meant that all the required data had to be supplied and any complimentary documentation had to be provided. Second, the applicant had to pay a fee to apply and obtain the certification. Sounds reasonable, right? This agency had a major problem: there were three types of certifications that could be obtained, and each type of certification was processed using a different application and hence was stored in one of three different databases! Even though most of the application information was the same or very similar for each applicant (e.g. applicant name, applicant address, and so on), each was stored in its own database. And to make matters worse, the payment information was kept in yet another database in a completely different department. I was part of a team of analysts that came into this agency and harmonized their disparate data sources, streamlined the application process (in this case by allowing electronic submission of a single application form), and cut the length of time from application to certification almost in half!

Inefficient processes are usually the product of poorly structured data and databases. This stands to reason because if you have to access multiple databases on different technology platforms in order to gather, process, and present information, the process itself and the poor data storage strategies will be equally to blame for your issues!

You might say, "So what? What's the harm as long as the work gets done and the reports go out the door on time?" Shame on you! I hope you're not saying that! Don't be lulled into complacency by the mere fact that the work is getting done and the reports are being delivered! The data contained in those reports is questionable, or worse, inaccurate. Accepting erroneous data as accurate and reliable exposes you and your client to many potential risks! For example, let's say you've just laid the concrete foundation of a structure, and you hire an engineer to test the stability of the walls. If the data regarding the soundness of the material is inaccurate, you may build your structure on a faulty foundation. Consider the risk of that scenario! The data provided in any situation needs to be structured, consolidated, accurate, and then made more reliable. This data needs to be harmonized.

The topic of analyzing and harmonizing data is not a new subject. Organizations at all levels and of all sizes have struggled with managing disparate data sources and maintaining multiple naming conventions as well as with a general lack of data reliability and standardization since long before computers came along.

There are many ways to systematically organize data. The process of data harmonization is not a new or complex process. In fact, it follows closely in principle with the process of normalization. If you have ever categorized or classified data into groups and then identified relationships between those groups, guess what? You've already performed data harmonization at a high level! But before you pat yourself on the back too hard, let's dive deeper into this process.

But before we launch into data harmonization and all its glory, let's talk about the concerns that arise by having and enabling stovepipe systems and silos of information. A stovepipe system is a computer system whose functionality and processes are narrowly focused to provide specific data to a specific recipient. I've already cited an example from my past experience earlier in this book (the government agency) in which time and resources were wasted due to information silos. I'm betting you have an example or two you could share as well.

ISSUES WITH INFORMATION SILOS

Generally speaking, here are some issues that every data analyst should be concerned with when confronted with disparate data sources:

- Redundancy: Data redundancy occurs when a data element is stored in more than one location or database at the same time. This creates issues with the reliability of the data being retrieved. Quite simply, the question becomes, *Which occurrence of the data is correct?*

- Authoritative data: This is "officially recognized data that can be certified and provided by an authoritative source." In other words, authoritative data is data that your organization provides and that is accepted by the consumer as reliable and accurate. If data is stored redundantly and/or must be converted in order to be presented, you are vulnerable to irregularities, mistakes, and errors.

- Stewardship: Data stewardship is the responsible management of all aspects of data and related metadata. In order for the data to be reliable, you must have a single point of contact (POC) for maintenance of the data and that POC should be a subject matter expert (or SME, pronounced "smee") for that specific data area. When multiple people update redundant data elements in multiple data stores, things quickly spiral out of control.

5

- Accessibility: Accessibility addresses the ability or authority to access, view, and update the data contained in the data stores. Accessibility should be restricted or constrained to only those persons who need access to the data. If one department can update the same data that is stored but restricted in another department, the data quickly becomes out of sync and inaccurate.

- Transfer: Data transfer issues arise when the format of data stored in the sending entity is not the same as the format in the receiving entity. There are methods for getting around such issues, including an interchange language such as eXtensible Markup Language (XML), but if the problem resides with the integrity of the data from the sending entity or the application of a conversion routine, not in the intermediate exchange technology, then XML is of little value as a transfer mechanism if the data that is transferred is wrong.

- Timeliness: Timeliness addresses the issue of retrieving the required data in a timeframe that allows the decision maker ample time to review, analyze, and make the correct decision based on accurate and reliable information. If the data has to be retrieved from several different data stores and then massaged, converted, and reformatted, chances are your stakeholder will not receive the information in a timely manner.

HOW DOES THIS HAPPEN?

The issues raised by stovepipe systems can be considered the lowlights of the IT department. All of the issues listed, plus other issues, potentially expose your client to risks; risks to their reputation and credibility, and even possible financial risks in certain situations. Data becomes stovepiped for many reasons: if response times are too slow for one department, data may be held redundantly for performance purposes; one person or department may require data that is slightly different than what was already contained in a data store; geographic considerations may play a role in separating the data; and I've even seen people download data from a department data store to a desktop application in order to manipulate the numbers and then label that spreadsheet a "system" or authoritative source.

No information technology organization is immune to unreliable and disparate data stores. Stovepipes tend to evolve over time and fly under the radar. They usually go unnoticed until a stakeholder makes a poor decision based on data that someone in the organization provided. That's when questions come up about where the data resides and who is maintaining it—but by then, it may be too late!

In many cases, the size of the business drives the accuracy and integrity of the data and the associated data stores. The data structures of small businesses tend to be smaller, more centralized, and accurate. They're simply holding less data. Generally speaking, the less voluminous the data, the easier it is to manage. As companies grow in size, complexity, and geographic diversity, the amount of data that they need to store and sustain themselves also rises. Heck, even the federal government is not impervious to the stovepipe predicament. In fact, the federal government is engaged in a very active campaign to break down the silos of information, consolidate data sources where possible, and start leveraging data as an enterprise asset, rather than an agency-controlled, locally owned possession.

Successful data harmonization provides a means for your clients and customers to interact and communicate using data and information that is reliable, not overlapping, wholly understood, and definable across all required organizational boundaries. By eliminating duplicative data that exists in multiple data stores, you'll realize substantial financial gains because you no longer must maintain the silos of information and their associated technology platforms.

You also eliminate the need for the conversion programs that were composed to convert one data element in one system format to an acceptable format in another data store. And don't forget the personnel side of the equation either. Once the data has been harmonized and consolidated, just think of all the additional time some of your employees will have in which to complete other, more important tasks in the organization.

AN EXAMPLE ORGANIZATION

One of the best ways to understand the data harmonization process is to look at an example. To that end, we will be following the data issues and activities of Monty's Import Service.

Let's first look at the corporate profile of Monty's Import Service:

- Monty's is a fairly small import operation that deals with imports only—no exports.

- Monty's only operates at three ports of entry that are passable by truck (land borders).

- Monty's clients regulate the importation of exactly ten commodities into the United States.

- Four of the ten commodities are categorized as perishable.

- Five of the ten commodities are categorized as nonperishable.

- One of the commodities is imported infrequently and doesn't fall into either of the other two categories.

So far, so good? Good! Let's continue.

In order to import products into the United States, importing companies have to submit import forms to Monty's Import Service to secure entry of the commodities across the borders in question. Here is a sample of the three forms utilized by Monty's Import Service:

Form 100-P: Permit to Import Perishable Goods

<table>
<tr><td>PHONE (360) 671-0125
FAX (360) 671-0126
E-MAIL Monty@mis.com</td><td colspan="2" align="center">**MONTY'S IMPORT SERVICE**
FORM 100-P</td><td>123 Border Drive
Bellingham, WA 98227</td></tr>
</table>

IMPORTER NAME AND ADDRESS		EXPORTER NAME AND ADDRESS		Arrival #	
				Arrival Date	
				Importer ID	

Port of Entry: **Port of Departure:** **Carrier Code:**

Description of Merchandise

MERCH CODE	TARIFF CODE	PACKAGE TYPE	VOLUME	COUNTRY OF ORIGIN		

SIGNATURES

Importer Signature		**Date**
M.I.S. Name		
M.I.S Signature		**Date**

10

Form 100-NP: Permit to Import Nonperishable Goods

PHONE (360) 671-0125	123 Border Drive
FAX (360) 671-0126	Bellingham, WA 98227
E-MAIL Monty@mis.com	

MONTY'S IMPORT SERVICE
FORM 100-NP

IMPORTER NAME		FOREIGN EXPORTER		Arrival No.	
IMPORTER ADDRESS		FOREIGN EXPORTER LOCATION		Date of Arrival	
				Importer Identifier	

| **Point of Entry:** | **Foreign Export Port:** | **Carrier:** |

Merchandise Description

COMMODITY IDENTIFIER	TARIFF CODE	PACKAGING	NUMBER OF PACKAGES	COUNTRY OF PRODUCTION	MERCHANDISE REMARKS		

SIGNATURES

Importer Signature		**Date**	
M.I.S. Name			
M.I.S Signature		**Date**	

Form 200-NC: Permit to Import Special Goods

| PHONE (360) 671-0125 FAX (360) 671-0126 E-MAIL Monty@mis.com | **MONTY'S IMPORT SERVICE** FORM 200-NC | 123 Border Drive Bellingham, WA 98227 |

NAME AND ADDRESS		OVERSEAS EXPORTER		Entrance Number	
		LOCATION OF OVERSEAS EXPORTER		Entrance Date	
				Importer Code	

Port of Entry:	Foreign Port:	Carrier Code:

Commodity Description

COMMODITY	TARIFF CODE	HOW PACKAGED?	AMOUNT	COUNTRY OF MANUFACTURE		

SIGNATURES

Importer Signature		Date	
M.I.S. Name			
M.I.S Signature		Date	

The three ports of entry that Monty's supervises are geographically diverse. One is in the state of Washington; another is in North Dakota; and the third is in Maine. And one last point to note: any of the ten products can be imported through any of the three ports of entry. (By the way, even though these points of entry are on land, they are still referred to as "ports" in import/export jargon.)

So as not to overcomplicate this example, let's assume that the business process is intact and working reasonably well for the import practice. The problem we're trying to solve lies mainly with the data and data storage, not with the business processes (although they may be at least partially to blame, and we will be reviewing them at a very high level).

As we progress in this book, I'll refer back to Monty's Import Service when necessary to help you gain a clearer understanding of how data analysis and harmonization function and how these methods can be practically applied to streamline data and make processes and overall operations more efficient.

SUMMARY

The inefficient collection, storage, and maintenance of corporate data in some organizations today can lead to multiple business issues over the course of time. Business processes that once were sound and performed effectively can become wrought with ineffective procedures, redundantly held data, and data sets that have serious integrity and accuracy anomalies.

Data harmonization seeks to rectify data redundancy, unclear authoritative data sources, poor data stewardship, inaccessibility of data, and a lack of timeliness. By harmonizing data stores, you will notice not only cleaner data but also easier and timelier access to more reliable data as well as time and resource savings due to streamlined business processes. Your data is the most important corporate asset that you or your client owns. You must manage it well!

CHAPTER 2

IDENTIFY THE DATA SOURCES

As I already mentioned, data harmonization is an iterative process. Remember, we are imagining that you have been hired by a client to analyze and consolidate their disparate data stores; so your initial effort for the harmonization process should be directed toward identifying all data that your client and your client's business processes (and possibly their stakeholders) require to make business decisions and successfully complete their existing (and possibly target) business processes. In short, you want to give them the data they need to do their jobs—when they need it and in a format that makes sense.

Let me point out that the same process can (and should) be followed when you're performing data harmonization *within* an organization—not just when you are a data consultant to a client. We want to focus on the tasks that need to be accomplished, the process to be followed, and the corresponding benefits; it doesn't matter whether you're a hired gun or an internal analyst.

GETTING STARTED ON THE DATA TRAIL

The best way to start gathering the required data is to identify all the forms that the client is using. These can be paper forms if it's a paper-based process or online forms if the submission of the forms is electronic. Regardless of whether it is electronic or paper-based (or a mix of both), your initial goal is to identify all the data that is contained in those forms. Each field on the forms will be identified as an individual data element. As you identify the data elements, record available peripheral data, or metadata, about each of the data elements identified on the forms. During this process, you should also identify relationships that exist between and among the data elements, as this information will be essential later in the harmonization process.

Metadata	Quite simply, metadata is data about data. It is data that describes the contents of information.
Data Element	A data element is an atomic unit of data that has precise meaning, usage, and business value to the entity that collects it.

As you are analyzing and dissecting each form (a process also known as "shredding" the form), also give close attention to the directions that accompany the form. The directions contain a wealth of information that guides the user regarding what information is entered into each block on the form and will help clarify each of the data elements in the context of the form.

Valuable pieces of metadata to identify in the forms and instructions include:

- mandatory and optional fields;

- contingent fields, which become required if a related field is populated;

- permitted values, which usually take the form of an enumerated list of codes; and/or values that are valid (or accepted) for this particular data element

- yes/no fields, commonly referred to as Boolean data elements, which take the values of *yes* or *no*, *on* or *off*, *checked* or *unchecked*, and so on;

- free-form text, which are unstructured fields and will likely end up being defined-size text fields;

- related documents, such as any additional or supplemental documentation that must also accompany the form or data, for example, a license number, a birth certificate, an authorization letter, etc.; and

- "other" fields, the dreaded categories that allow users to make choices that are not available in the lists of permitted values enumerated for individual data elements (Generally, a user selects "other" and then must populate a related text field with the exception/ explanation; this is an example of a contingent field, as mentioned earlier).

HIT CYBERSPACE: CHECK THE WEB

Once you've analyzed the forms, your next area of data analysis will be the company website. Virtually every company, regardless of size, has a website. And that website will likely be chock-full of information about the company, its lines of business, expertise, clients, history, staff, and leadership. This is all information in the public domain that is ripe for ingesting!

Here are some potentially helpful items to identify as you're reviewing the website:

- Company charter and mission: Why is the organization in

business? What type of footprint does it hope to leave on its industry? Who is the primary beneficiary of the company's services?

- Nomenclature: Learn as much as you can about the jargon of your client's industry. This will help bring the data into a coherent context and help you more clearly discuss issues with your client.

- Downloads: Review the information that is available for download, such as process manuals, portfolio information, newsletters, and so on; any literature published by the company may be a valuable resource for you.

- Recent activities: What has the company done in the last week? Last month? Last six months? Will recent activities have an impact on your analysis or create additional data requirements now or in the future?

- News releases: These will generally highlight how the client has positively impacted its industry. You'll find that the company website will accentuate the positive and severely downplay the negative; but you'll want to collect both types of information.

- Strategic plan: This identifies the future strategic direction of the company and can give you a head start on determining future data that may be required.

- Industry mandates: Identify governing bodies that regulate your client's industry as a whole and your client's actions in particular; attempt to become very familiar with these administrators.

- Calendar: This may provide information on training courses, consortiums, corporate events, conferences hosted or attended, and so on. If possible, begin to attend events at which your client is a key player.

- Newsletter: Sign up for the company newsletter. These are usually free of charge and will enable you to keep abreast of company activities, even when you cannot access the company website.

Please realize that each company will have a different level of sophistication, and the company website will likely reflect that. Remember, the website is just another resource in your search for relevant data!

CHAT 'EM UP: TALK TO THE EXPERTS

Okay, now that you have combed the forms, reviewed the website, and read all the relevant materials, you are now ready to meet with and interview the experts at the client site. You will want to work closely with your technical point of contact to identify all potential subject matter experts (SMEs), managers, and users of the data that you're analyzing (plus other stakeholders, if required). Don't take these interviews lightly! The information you garner from these technical interviews will likely corroborate the data you've already gathered and, more important, expose data that you had no idea existed.

The first step in this interview process is setting up an interview schedule. This is extremely important! Your clients are likely very busy people, so keep your interview times reasonable and be flexible on dates, times, and locations. The employees at the client company are the experts (and the client is paying the bill), so be available and when possible, work around their schedules and conduct interviews at their office. If a SME is in his or her own office, he or she will be much more comfortable and will also have easy access to documentation that is stored there.

Select as many individuals as necessary to get as complete a picture of the business processes and data as you can. This will likely be driven and constrained by resources, money, and time. Ideally, you'll want to interview someone who represents a horizontal, crosscut of the company at a high level—possibly the operational manager or chief information officer (CIO)—as well as mid-level persons at the company who will likely be the number crunchers and report producers and thus will be extremely familiar with the data. If possible, interview some of the frontline workers too. These are the employees who work with the data day in and day out and will be familiar with some of the informal avenues of data exchange and collection (yes, the proverbial "sneakernet" does still exist). These workers will also be knowledgeable of some of the data anomalies and quirks.

Let's take a moment to discuss the types of interviews that you should consider. There are many methods of interviewing clients, such as face-to-face, over the phone, and by video conferencing, just to name a few. Then there is the decision of whether to interview people one-on-one or in groups. Facilitated sessions and joint application design (JAD) sessions are also options. My experience has been that one-on-one or one-on-two interviewing works best, particularly with high-level interviewees. If you must interview more than one person at a time, I would recommend limiting the number of client personnel to three. This allows you to get information from multiple sources but also allows for consensus building when different information or opinions are presented or expressed. Utilize facilitated or JAD sessions for large groups (eight or more). The focus of the large-group discussions should center on late-lifecycle artifacts like business process diagramming and functional requirements gathering.

Once you've set up your interview schedule, your next step will be to compose your interview questions and draft those questions and discussion points into a document. Create the amount and number of questions for the interview while keeping in mind the scheduled amount of time so you are able to get through all the questions in the allotted time. Be prepared to send the questions to the interviewees prior to actually sitting down with them. This will give them the opportunity to compose answers and ask for clarification if necessary. By doing this, you can streamline the interview process and take less time, which will translate to a happier client!

Below are a few sample questions, discussion points, and recommendations for conducting your interview. This is by no means meant to be an exhaustive listing, but these recommendations have worked well for me in the past:

- Always record the time, date, and location of each interview. Trust me on this—you won't remember these details in a month.

- Always record relevant information about each interviewee, including name, position or title, the organization or office he or she works in, and his or her primary role or job description.

- Identify what corporate data is collected, how it is collected, and where it is stored; think interface specifications: commercial off-the-shelf (COTS) products versus in-house developed systems, so-called sneakernets, and even CD and thumb drive delivery modes.

- Identify the primary stakeholders, what data they receive, and how they receive it.

- Identify any known or conjectured risks as they relate to data. For example, if the system goes down, are there secondary transmission means?

- What instruments are in place to control data dissemination? Identify any memoranda of understanding (MOUs) or memoranda of agreement (MOAs), commercial contracts, and data dumps.

- Start many questions with the phrase "List all the _____." (You will fill in the applicable terms depending on what information you are seeking.)

- Avoid asking yes/no questions unless they are necessary for verification. Open-ended questions provide more information and naturally lead to more open and fruitful discussion.

- Always finish interviews with a discussion of how the data can be improved. This will give each interviewee a chance to express discontent as well as have a voice in future improvements in the data or processes.

- Be sure that you thank the interviewees profusely! They are taking time out of their busy schedules to speak with you; be very gracious.

- Last, I highly recommend that at least two analysts (you and another person) be present during each interview. It is very difficult for one person to facilitate an interview, elicit detailed information, and accurately record the comments, answers, and remarks. Bring a second person to act as a scribe.

SEND A SURVEY

In cases where there is a need to garner information from the actual users of the reports that your client produces, it may be more economical to compose a survey and distribute it to the clientele. This method is particularly useful when the end users of the information are geographically dispersed. Although nothing replaces speaking with someone face-to-face, answers to survey questions can still provide valuable input for your data analysis.

To get the best responses from a survey, make it as easy and painless as possible for the person taking the survey. Your best bet is to make the survey available on a website and easily accessible via any Web-enabled software. The survey should be as short as possible while still capable of obtaining all the information you require.

The following are a few sample questions and discussion points you may want to include in a data-user survey:

- List all the reports currently received from the company.

- What specific pieces of data are of the most interest to you?

- How often do you receive reports?

- Is data missing from these reports? Is it accurate and correctly formatted?

- How extensively is the data processed after it is received (if it is processed at all)?

- Ask the survey respondents to provide details and examples when appropriate. Build text boxes into the survey for this purpose.

- Thank respondents for their time and expertise.

- Make sure respondents submit the surveys once they've completed them!

I know the last bullet point seems like a no-brainer, but the last thing you want is for a respondent to take the time and energy to complete the survey and log out of the session without saving and submitting their responses. Most users will not be willing to complete the survey a second time if this happens.

REVIEW THE CURRENT SYSTEM DOCUMENTATION

Once your initial analysis, interviews, and surveys are complete, you should have quite a bit of input to sift through. But the last piece of the data puzzle, and another valuable source of data, is the current system documentation. This may be scant or voluminous depending on how large the company is, how large the system or systems are, the age of the system or systems, and how diligent the company has been in maintaining its documentation. Details on the current system documentation will be available from many of the sources we have already discussed. For example, user manuals may have been downloaded from the corporate website or provided to you by the SMEs whom you interviewed. The database administrator (DBA) may have even given you a dump of the data definition language (DDL). Conceptual, logical, and physical models are great sources of data, metadata, and the relationships that govern the maintenance of that data. By all means, obtain copies of any or all of these artifacts if possible.

The sheer volume of raw data may seem daunting at this point, but don't be overwhelmed. We will soon review how you can systematically sort, group, and harmonize all of this data into an artifact that is much more comprehendible, comprehensive, concise, and useful.

THOUGHT POINTS

I must raise several important points that will be valuable to you at this stage of the data analysis and harmonization.

1. Gather all the information that you possibly can. I cannot stress this enough. If the client is willing to make relevant materials available—even if they seem only marginally related at the present time—take them! Make a determination of their value and relevance later in your analysis.

2. It is easier to reduce the amount of assembled information than it is to gather additional artifacts. In other words, collect as much information as possible at the outset and then weed out materials that are not relevant or not needed for your data analysis as you progress through the harmonization process. This brings me to my last point ...

3. Learn as much as you can about your client's business, organization, and industry. You will accumulate an abundance of facts and information as you complete your analysis and interviews and compile your survey results. Not all of these facts will be directly relevant for data analysis, but these artifacts will contribute to your overall depth of knowledge of the client and industry and will come in handy when you are in discussions with SMEs and asking industry-related questions.

Your client will appreciate your thorough analysis. I will tell you from experience, many clients detest having to explain a point that you should already know from doing diligent background research. In the same vein, you will find them getting frustrated when asked questions that they have already answered. Cover all your data bases (pun intended); be prepared to talk to someone in a particular industry in their own terms.

SUMMARY

There are numerous resources that you can leverage and exploit in order to gather as much information as possible about the client's data and processes. You also want to pull together the peripheral data, the metadata, and the relationships between the elements as you're performing the analysis. Among the resources we've discussed are the forms (paper or online), the company website, SME interviews, surveys, and current system documentation such as data models and process manuals.

Keep in mind that one of your main goals at this stage of data analysis is to identify and gather as much information and documentation as possible. Even if the information appears peripheral presently, record it and analyze its relevance later in the process.

CHAPTER 3

REVIEWING THE DATA STANDARDS

No data analysis discussion would be complete without talking about industry-wide data standards that are prevalent in and across many businesses and organizations. These standards determine the manner in which data is collected, stored, and transmitted between organizations that exist within the same or different industries. We have spoken at length about learning the details of your client's industry because it gives you a firm context in which to analyze the data and processes. Now let's examine the relationship between the data you'll collect and harmonize and the national and international standards that exist to govern it.

Many of these industry standards were created in order to facilitate the exchange of data and information between systems, computers, industries, and individuals who are dealing in the same general category of data. A realistic example of meaningful data exchange would be a county law enforcement agency requesting data from a federal data source on a suspect who was just detained. The source data (from the federal law enforcement agency) will be stored in data structures that are quite different from the data schemas of the requesting agency (the county law enforcement agency). By applying industry standards to the data, these two agencies, existing at differing levels of bureaucracy, can exchange similar data even though each has a different data framework. The exchanges are performed in such a way as to allow the data to maintain its meaning, context, and integrity regardless of the transmitting and receiving parties. When the data is aligned with a specific data standard, it is said to be *conformant, compliant* or *well formed*, depending on the standard that is applied.

DATA STANDARD EXAMPLES AND CONSIDERATIONS

Let's discuss several of these standards, models, and frameworks. You, as a data analyst, may want to align your HDS (harmonized data set) with a model or framework that works for you and your client.

- NIEM: The National Information Exchange Model is "designed to develop, disseminate and support enterprise-wide information exchange standards and processes that can enable jurisdictions to effectively share critical information in emergency situations, as well as support the day-to-day operations of agencies throughout the nation." The NIEM was developed through a partnership between the US Department of Justice (DOJ) and the Department of Homeland Security (DHS). "The NIEM exchange development methodology results in a common semantic understanding among participating organizations and data formatted in a semantically consistent manner." In other words, it provides a medium that standardizes the actual data content of transmissions. Although the NIEM was developed to enhance communications between federal government agencies, it has expanded to include data types that can be utilized by nongovernment agencies, commercial entities, and health care administrators. If your client deals in law enforcement or health care, you may want to consider examining the NIEM data models and methodologies and aligning your harmonized data set with that of the NIEM.

- WCO: The World Customs Organization is aimed exclusively at international Customs matters and regulations. "The WCO is recognized as the voice of the global Customs community. It is particularly noted for its work in areas covering the development of global standards, the simplification and harmonization of Customs procedures, trade supply chain security, the facilitation of international trade, the enhancement of Customs enforcement and compliance activities." The WCO maintains a very extensive collection of data models, standards, metadata, and frameworks, each dedicated to facilitating the exchange of customs-related data to enhance the global trade process. If your client deals with importing or exporting commodities, you may want to consider examining the WCO data framework and aligning your harmonized data set with that of the WCO. In a fairly recent development, NIEM and the WCO have decided to collaborate on data standards, and NIEM has actually subsumed the WCO data and frameworks.

- ISO: The International Organization for Standardization is "the world's largest developer and publisher of International Standards." The ISO provides standardized listings of terminology used to describe everything from mathematics and natural sciences to information technology, agriculture, and military engineering. One of the goals of the ISO is to facilitate "a state of industry-wide standardization." This means that "stakeholders agree on specifications and criteria to be applied consistently in the classification of materials, in the manufacture and supply of products, in testing and analysis, in terminology and in the provision of services. In this way, International Standards provide a reference framework, or a common technological language, between suppliers and their customers. This facilitates trade and the transfer of technology." If your client is a member of ISO (the United States is an active member) or elects to be ISO compliant in its data conventions, then you may consider doing additional research on ISO to ascertain if this is a viable option.

- ANSI: The American National Standards Institute "oversees the creation, promulgation and use of thousands of norms and guidelines that directly impact businesses in nearly every sector." ANSI asserts to achieve this "by promoting and facilitating voluntary consensus standards and conformity assessment systems, and safeguarding their integrity." ANSI is the official US representative to the ISO and is comprised of a multitude of different government agencies, academic institutions, and individuals— approximately 3.5 million members strong. The mission of ANSI is focused on "...further improving U.S. competitiveness abroad while continuing to provide strong support for domestic markets and the American quality of life." If your client is competitive in this line of business (LOB) or active in this community of interest (COI), you may want to consider aligning with the ANSI.

- FIPS: The Federal Information Processing Standards "[approve] standards and guidelines that are developed by the National Institute of Standards and Technology (NIST) for Federal computer systems. These standards and guidelines are issued by NIST as Federal Information Processing Standards (FIPS) for use government-wide. NIST develops FIPS when there are compelling Federal government requirements such as for security and interoperability and there are no acceptable industry standards or solutions." In addition, "the major focus of NIST activities in information technology is developing tests, measurements, proofs of concept, reference data and other technical tools to support the development of pivotal, forward-looking technology." For example, there are FIPS listings for country codes, region codes, and state codes. There are also FIPS standards for encoding and encrypting data. Once again, consider what line of business your client is in and align your harmonized data set accordingly.

- FEA DRM: The Federal Enterprise Architecture Data Reference Model, in conjunction with the four accompanying FEA reference models, seeks to "facilitate cross-agency analysis and the elimination of duplicative investments, gaps and opportunities for collaboration within and across Federal Agencies." Furthermore, "the DRM describes, at an aggregate level, the data and information supporting government programs and business line operations. This model enables agencies to describe the types of interaction, data and exchanges occurring between the Federal government and citizens." The FEA DRM, along with the other models, is used heavily in the federal government to facilitate and govern the exchange of data across agency and organizational boundaries. If your client is working closely with the Federal government, or your client is the federal government itself, you will need to acquaint your data analysts with the Federal Enterprise Architecture framework.

This is by no means an exhaustive list of standards, guidelines, and frameworks. There are many, many standards that exist to enforce numerous and diverse industries. For example, in the biological community, the Biodiversity Information Standards, formerly known as the Taxonomic Database Working Group (TDWG), "focuses on the development of standards for the exchange of biological/biodiversity data." In the health care area, the Healthcare Information Technology Standards Panel (HITSP) "was formed for the purpose of harmonizing and integrating standards that will meet clinical and business needs for sharing information among organizations and systems." Although, the standards I have mentioned here are used for guiding entire industries, there are data standards in place at the state and local levels as well. You may need to become familiar with these and align to them instead.

As discussed above, some industries have rigorous standards to which members of those industries must adhere. By having knowledge of these structures and guidelines, as well as the mandates that enabled them, you can integrate these standards into your data analysis. Bear in mind that the particular industry you are analyzing may adhere to more than one standard. Don't be surprised if the industry you're working in is governed by multiple data standards at different levels. In this case, embrace the standards and allow them to work collaboratively to align the harmonized data to the identified standard or standards.

SUMMARY

Every good data analyst should be aware of the data standards that are prevalent in the industry in question. As was pointed out, there are different standards that align themselves with particular lines of business and specific communities of interest. But there are also standards that span entire industries and provide regulation and direction to all organizations within those industries. For example, the NIEM standard seeks to assert a standard template for data exchange spanning multiple industries, whereas the WCO is aimed exclusively at the exchange of data relating to international customs matters. Your client's line of business will dictate which of the standards you should align to.

CHAPTER 4

MANAGING THE DATA

You are now sitting at your desk staring at piles of forms, interview notes, comments, models, survey results, and industry standards. You have all this information that you've gathered and elicited from all the right people ... Now what?

Well, now it's time to consolidate all the facts, figures, and meaningful information. The goal at this stage is to get all the data and metadata into one central repository. Just as we're helping our client eliminate redundant data and create single-sourced, authoritative information, we also need to bring together all our disparate pieces of information into a single, centralized location.

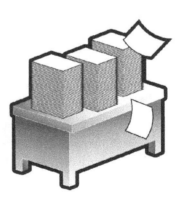

DATA MANAGEMENT TOOLS

It's time to talk about using a tool to help manage all this information in a coherent, efficient, and comprehensive fashion. Don't just start recording data in a spreadsheet or Word document;

you'll quickly find the task will grow beyond and overwhelm the capabilities of these software programs. You will need to select a tool that is specifically designed to capture data requirements and the metadata associated with the captured data elements. There are many good tools that can help you right out of the box, but there are specific features you'll want to look for to identify the right tool. Let's go tool shopping!

The first place to search for a good data management tool is in your own organization. Make a few phone calls and send out a few e-mails to your software support team and find out if your company already has a license for any data requirements management software. You may be surprised to find that your company already has active licenses sitting out on the server that were purchased for other similar projects. Use them!

If no software is available internally, another option is to investigate whether your company has a partnership with any software companies that own data management software tools and will allow you to use the software for free or at least purchase the software at a reduced price.

If you're fortunate enough to have software in-house or easily available from a partner, here are some considerations to bear in mind:

- Version and release: Check which version of the software is available (for purchase or in-house). If the software was purchased a year or more ago, chances are there is a new version or release of the software currently available. If possible, arrange for your copy to be upgraded. Generally, if you have a maintenance contract in place (and it hasn't expired), an upgrade is free or nominally priced.

- Compatibility: Ensure compatibility between the version of the software that resides on the server and the version of the software that is installed on your desktop. Believe it or not, some client-side installations are not upwardly or downwardly compatible with the server-side version of the same software if only one side of the configuration has been upgraded. This has happened to me!

- Tool knowledge and training: Another consideration in selecting a tool is whether someone in your organization knows how to use the tool effectively. If you or any member of your team is not familiar with the tool, then you will need to investigate training classes or bringing in a contractor to get you started, trained, and moving forward.

- Spreadsheets: I have already mentioned this, but it bears repeating: do not use a spreadsheet to manage your data analysis and requirements. A spreadsheet does not have the power to handle the volume of data you'll be entering into it, nor does it have valuable features such as traceability or impact analysis that will be necessary later in the life cycle. Also, you'll soon be doing some serious number crunching and data manipulation; these capabilities are a big part of the harmonization process and need to be planned for now.

If you have no data management software tool in-house or via a partnership, don't panic. The next place to turn is to your client. Your client may already have a data management software in mind for you to use. Many times, your client will already be using a particular software and will leave you no choice in which software to use. The decision is determined by the statement of work (SOW). In some cases, your client may actually be directing you to not only identify the data requirements, but also recommend a software or software suite to use. Read the SOW carefully to determine the situation you're in before you start entering the gathered information into a tool.

If all else fails, you may find yourself in a position of having to purchase a tool to get the job done. This is not as bad as it seems! Keep in mind, you're not only selecting a tool for the present analysis and project at hand, but you are potentially making a long-term investment in technology. You also must consider future functionality and longevity of the tool. Identify other projects that could possibly benefit by using the tool; this will help build consensus on which tool to select. Last, remember to investigate the maintenance agreement, purchase restrictions, and renewal fees for the software (the so-called fine print). These will vary widely from vendor to vendor. This is no easy task, but it is a task that needs to be completed nonetheless.

ADDITIONAL TOOL FEATURES

Some further considerations and functions you may want to evaluate when selecting a tool are below:

- Reporting: Any tool that you select should have a very strong reporting capability. One of the goals of data harmonization is to clearly communicate the discovered data requirements to your client. You must be able to extract that information from the selected tool easily and accurately and present it in a variety of ways, including graphically.

- Ad hoc and canned: Most commercial software will contain "canned" reports; these are reports that the vendor has created and loaded into the software. These are usually reports that the vendor has determined are used most by clients who purchase this software. Occasionally, a canned report just won't provide the data that you need for a specific report or data call. In this situation, the tool must be flexible and robust enough to handle ad hoc queries for data.

- Accessibility: The tool that you choose should have the capability of restricting access to critical or sensitive data, or at the very least allowing an administrator to set up roles with different authority levels and access to the data. This will become increasingly important when multiple analysts need to access different sections of the same data, so, for example, one person can be reviewing the data in "read only" mode while another person has the data "locked" for update.

- Scalability: This is one of the most overused terms in IT, but in this case it is very applicable. The tool you choose must be able to gracefully handle increased or expanded amounts of data and functionality without considerable retooling, upgrading, or intervention. One of the goals of working with any client should be securing more work with that client. You don't want to have to run through the whole tool selection process again, right?

- Integration: Many of the data management tools available are only one tool included in a larger software suite. Since the same company has created the software, all the modules fit together well and play nicely with one another. Investigate whether the tool you select will integrate (or communicate) with software from other vendors. This is important because not all software will readily and easily transfer data without a conversion process as a go-between. This can cause significant financial and resource issues down the road.

- Web access: Most of the data management tools that I have worked with have web-based components that allow your client to access and view reports that have been published to the web. This can save you a lot of time and money if your client requests various reports on a frequent basis. Instead of creating the report and sending the client a huge file, you can execute the query and expose the report to a secure web page; then your client can log in and get the data needed in a fraction of the time!

- Traceability: Further along in the software life cycle, you'll be using the results of the data harmonization work in conjunction with other artifacts such as business processes, use cases, and table definitions. The tool you choose should allow you to relate, or link, one type of artifact (or object) to another. By doing so, you will be able to determine what impact a change in one artifact (say, a data element) will have on another, related artifact, such as a use case. Impact analysis will become important when you begin relating data requirements to functional requirements.

What you're looking for in a data management tool is a flexible instrument that will assist you in your data gathering and management, plus make your data analysis work easier and more successful. To that end, the chosen tool must be able to manipulate the data that is entered into it. It should have robust grouping and sorting capability. It should support impact analysis, and, as already mentioned, it should be able to assist you when you're creating reports or pulling together presentations. There are many tools out there, so do your homework!

Regardless of the tool you choose, you will reap numerous benefits by entering all your analysis and data into one tool and centralizing it to one controlled, easily accessible location.

THOUGHT POINTS

I'd like to make a few recommendations for you to consider during this early point in the data harmonization process. A data analyst at this stage of the game should keep the following ideas in mind:

1. You are gathering the "what" at this point, that is, the data elements and the metadata. In the early stages of data harmonization, you want to gather data and information in somewhat of a vacuum. Keep your scope tight and your business process analysis at a minimum! There will be plenty of opportunity to shred the business processes later in the life cycle.

2. While you're gathering information, you will inevitably discover business rules that apply to the data elements that you have recorded. Make note of them, and then leave them alone. Don't get caught up in considering when and where business rules should be applied; it will severely hamper your ability to objectively gather and harmonize the data. You can (and will) deal with business rules at a later point.

3. Last, please leave the word "how" out of your data harmonization vocabulary. In other words, don't ask questions like "How will this be implemented?" or "How will we design this?" You are collecting data and data requirements; don't cloud the issue with design. Design and eventual development will be done by another person or team later in the life cycle.

SUMMARY

Deciding which data management tool will be used on your project is extremely important. Start your research by checking in your own backyard; the company may already have licensed copies of data management software at its disposal. You should also be sure to review any partnerships with software companies and vendors. Remember to keep in mind considerations, such as version compatibility, in-house tool knowledge, and available training. Further data management functionalities to consider include:

- reporting

- accessibility

- scalability

- traceability

- ease of integration (into existing platforms and technologies)

The time and money you invest in tool selection and implementation at this stage will pay dividends, not only for the current project, but also for other similar projects in the future. There are many capable tools available, so do your research thoroughly.

Chapter 5

Start Harmonizing the Data

Let's quickly review where we are in the data analysis and harmonization process. We have identified all relevant forms and data elements. We have additional information from the website. We have interview notes, user manuals, and data models from the client SMEs, and we have made a decision regarding which tool to use to manage all this data. Now, we have to enter all the data and metadata into this single tool.

In chapter 1, we were introduced to Monty's Import Service and also were able to review the forms Monty's uses to collect data in the course of doing business. Let's imagine that at this point the forms have been shredded, and below are listings of all the data elements that have been gathered for analysis and harmonization. I have intentionally omitted the associated metadata and additional comments; we'll be using that portion of the analysis very shortly. For now, just review the raw list of data from the forms.

Form 100-P	Form 100-NP	Form 200-NC
Arrival Date	Date of Arrival	Entrance Date
Arrival Number	Arrival Number	Entrance Number
Name of Importer	Importer Name	Name
Address of Importer	Importer Address	Address
Importer Number	Importer Identifier	Importer Code
Carrier Code	Carrier	Carrier Code
Name of Foreign Exporter	Foreign Exporter	Overseas Exporter
Country of Foreign Exporter	Foreign Exporter Location	Location of Overseas Exporter
Country of Origin	Country of Production	Country of Manufacture
Port of Departure	Foreign Export Port	Foreign Port
Port of Entry	Point of Entry	Port of Entry
Description of Merchandise	Merchandise Description	Commodity Description
Merchandise Code	Commodity Identifier	Commodity
Tariff Code	Tariff Code	Tariff Code
Package Type	Packaging	How packaged?
Volume of Commodity	Number of Packages	Amount
Importer Signature	Merchandise Remarks	Importer Signature
Importer Signature Date	Importer Signature	Importer Signature Date
Monty's Import Service Official Name	Importer Signature Date	Monty's Import Service Official Name
Monty's Import Service Signature	Monty's Import Service Official Name	Monty's Import Service Signature
Monty's Import Service Signature Date	Monty's Import Service Signature	Monty's Import Service Signature Date
	Monty's Import Service Signature Date	

The most obvious opportunities for data harmonization are found in the repeating of data elements that have the same or similar definitions but are labeled differently. This is the proverbial low-hanging fruit for a data analyst. Let's look at some examples from our listing.

If we start at the top of the list, we see our first opportunity for harmonizing the data. On Form 100-NP, the Date of Arrival is recorded. On Form 100-P, we are recording the same piece of data, only we're calling it Arrival Date. We know these two elements represent the same piece of data because we have the definition in the metadata and, of course, because of the obvious similarities in the name alone. Here is a subset of your data analysis:

Data Element	Description	Form	Domain	Comments
Arrival Date	The date on which the conveyance crosses the border into the United States	100-P	Date	Format: MM/DD/YYYY
Date of Arrival	The date on which a truck crosses into the Continental United States	100-NP	Date	Should always equal Current Date

But, what happens when we introduce a third data element into the analysis? On Form 200-NC, the same data element is described yet another way: Entrance Date.

Now, we have to ask ourselves a question: is Entrance Date the date on which the commodity entered the United States, or is it the date on which the commodity entered the commerce of the United States? We can find the answer in the metadata that we so diligently gathered at the outset. Let's have a look:

Data Element	Description	Form	Domain	Comments
Arrival Date	The date on which the conveyance crosses the border into the United States	100-P	Date	Format: MM/DD/YYYY
Date of Arrival	The date on which a truck crosses into the Continental United States	100-NP	Date	Should always equal Current Date
Entrance Date	The date on which the vehicle crossed into US territory	200-NC	Date	Format: YYYY-MM-DD

As we compare the definitions, we can easily determine that, yes, the Entrance Date is the same data as the Arrival Date and the Date of Arrival. Note too that we have captured some valuable formatting information in our analysis and recorded it in the comments column for later usage.

Wow! So, instead of holding three different data elements (dates, in this case) that represent the same activity or object of data, we can harmonize those three data elements into one data element to represent all three disparate elements.

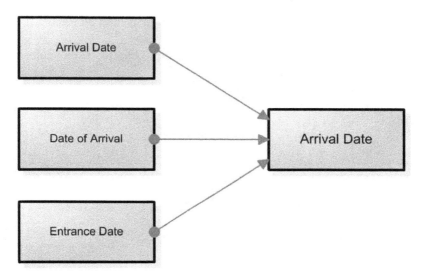

As you harmonize the data elements, you must be sure to keep careful notes on what the pieces of data represent, the lineage of the data (i.e., Which form does this data relate to?), and any formatting (domain, length, etc.) that is mentioned in your research. Additionally, as you consolidate the data elements, move them off the physical paper and into your data requirements management tool. By doing so, we can start eliminating some of the clutter and more easily manage our workload and process.

Let's harmonize another set of data elements from the three forms. This time let's review an element that is not so obvious: the information that represents the importer. In this example, we have Importer Identifier from Form 100-NP, Importer Number from Form 100-P, and Importer Code from Form 200-NC. Unlike our previous example dealing with the arrival date, this data element will require some analysis because, on the face, we cannot say absolutely that Importer Identifier, Importer Number, and Importer Code represent the same or similar objects. This is where your research of metadata and SME interviews will come in handy. There is no need to guess or speculate—the information is in your grasp!

Let's go straight to the definitions of these data elements.

Data Element	Description	Form	Domain	Length	Comments
Importer Identifier	A sequence of characters uniquely identifying the importer	100-NP	Alpha	9	
Importer Number	A number representing the entity acting as importer	100-P	Numeric	9	
Importer Code	A code designating the party acting in the role of importer	200-NC	Alpha	5	SME Interviews: valid codes for this element in table IMPORTER_CDS

By reviewing the metadata, we can again say with certainty that each Importer Identifier, Importer Number, and Importer Code clearly represents and identifies one unique importer who is performing the import task. The use of the word "code" in the identification of the importer raises an interesting point: If the importer populating the form is entering a code that represents his or her import firm, then we may need to maintain a list of valid importer codes. Furthermore, if Monty's Import Service only works with a select few importers, then we can maintain a finite, enumerated list of values. This will not only simplify the data entry process but also maintain consistency in the data values being stored. This is exactly the type of information we've already collected during our SME interviews and discussions. However, if the codes are not listed anywhere in your research and analysis, note this issue as one that you may later clarify with a SME.

So, now you are merrily reviewing the data elements from each form and harmonizing data like there's no tomorrow—but, wait! What if you can't harmonize a data element? What then? This scenario will occur often. Not all data elements will fall neatly in place and be easily harmonized. In fact, on very large projects, you could realistically be reviewing thousands of data elements, and you will very likely end up with a few "loners" and "orphans." This is not uncommon.

If you look back at our list, you'll see a data element called Merchandise Remarks that is captured on Form 100-NP. Neither Form 100-P or 200-NC contains a field that is comparable to or representative of Merchandise Remarks. In this situation, you must record the data element because it appears on a form used by Monty's Import Service, but you will also want to do a little research. For example, start finding answers to questions like these: Is this field always populated? Sometimes populated? Never populated? Is this field only entered if another field is entered? How long is this field? What type of information is generally entered? You can ask these questions of your client or review your meeting minutes to find the answers. If you find numerous loners, it may signal the need for further meetings to resolve the issues. The very fact that the element exists means that we have to account for it, but it may not end up as part of the finished product. In other words, if this field is never populated, then we need to analyze whether we're going to retain it or not. The entry into the tool may look something like this:

Data Element	Description	Form	Domain	Comments
Merchandise Remarks	Information relevant to the shipment or product	100-NP	Text	Free-form text field; determine what this field contains, when used, etc.

ABSTRACT HARMONIZING

There will be cases in which harmonizing data elements may require you to do some abstract thinking, such as when you analyze some of the more conceptual data elements like quantities and amounts. In fact, let's take a look at the data elements that represent the amount or volume of product being imported.

We have Number of Packages recorded on Form 100-NP, Volume of Commodity entered on Form 100-P, and Amount on Form 200-NC. The difficulty in this scenario lies in attempting to account for all the possible qualifiers for a given volume or amount. By "qualifier," I mean, for instance, the number of cans in a nonperishable shipment or the number of crates in a perishable shipment. In other words, don't we need to know the type of container to account for how much of it is being imported? Actually, no—we don't. Let me explain. By abstracting the volume, amount, count, or total to a higher level of identification, we can discern that all of these labels represent pieces of data describing quantity or, if you like, shipped quantity. At this stage, we are not interested in isolating the type of measurement; we are only concerned with recording that a quantity of *something* is being imported. Again, you'll want to note all the possible types, which will likely be transformed into an enumerated list later in the life cycle. But, during data harmonization, you are gathering the "what," in this case, quantity.

Identifying all the possible types, as I mentioned earlier, will give you a second opportunity for abstracting and harmonizing the data. If you take a step back and list all the types of containers that can hold commodities, both perishable and nonperishable, the list could get pretty large very quickly. There are cans, crates, bales, boxes, barrels, sacks, and pallets, just to name a few. But again, by abstracting these holding units, we can determine that all the possible holding units are really containers. Each holding unit contains something. So, at the abstract, logical level, we have a quantity of containers being imported on any given shipment. Remember to record all the types of containers for later use in the life cycle. Keep in mind that Monty's Import Service only deals with ten items, so the list will be easy to assemble.

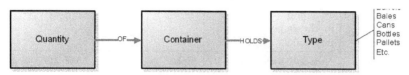

Once you have harmonized all the data, you should input all the data into the data requirements management tool that you selected earlier. Enter all the harmonized data elements and as much metadata as possible. Also, enter the other pieces of data, such as code lists and loners, that you uncovered during data analysis and harmonization. By this point, you'll also have identified risks and relationships that need to be recorded as well. Once all the data is entered, you can begin sorting and categorizing the harmonized data for ease of review, presentation, and clarification.

Below is the list of harmonized data elements for Monty's Import Service, including metadata.

Data Element	Description	Form	Domain	Length	Comments
Arrival Date	The date on which the conveyance crosses the border into the United States	100-P, 100-NP, 200-NC	Date	8	Format: MM/DD/YYYY
Arrival Number	An assigned number that identifies an import transaction	100-P, 100-NP, 200-NC	Numeric	9	Sequential numbering scheme

Importer Name	The registered name of the entity acting as importer in the import transaction	100-P, 100-NP, 200-NC	Text	30	
Importer Address	The physical address of the entity acting as importer in the import transaction	100-P, 100-NP, 200-NC	Text	60	Includes street, city, state, and postal code
Importer Code	A code which uniquely identifies an importer	100-P, 100-NP, 200-NC	Alpha	9	SME Interviews; valid codes for this element in table IMPORTER_CDS
Carrier Code	A code which uniquely identifies the transporter of the goods	100-P, 100-NP, 200-NC	Alpha	5	Valid codes for this element available on http://www.mis.com/cc.
Exporter Name	The registered name of the entity acting as exporter in the import transaction	100-P, 100-NP, 200-NC	Text	30	
Exporter Location	The country of residence for the entity acting as exporter in the import transaction	100-P, 100-NP, 200-NC	Text	3	Values are standard ISO Country Codes, for example: GRC = Greece
Origin Country Code	A code that identifies the country where the product was produced, manufactured, grown, etc.	100-P, 100-NP, 200-NC	Text	3	Values are standard ISO Country Codes, for example: GRC = Greece

Departure Port Code	A code that uniquely identifies the foreign port from which the shipment departed	100-P, 100-NP, 200-NC	Numeric	4	Values are identical to TSA listing.
Entry Port Code	A code that uniquely identifies the domestic port at which the shipment crosses into the United States	100-P, 100-NP, 200-NC	Numeric	4	Values are identical to TSA listing.
Commodity Code	A code that uniquely identifies the product being imported	100-P, 100-NP, 200-NC	Alpha	10	Internal list
Tariff Code	A code that classifies the commodity using the international tariff nomenclature	100-P, 100-NP, 200-NC	Numeric	10	Source: Harmonized tariff schedule
Container Type Code	A code that identifies type of enclosure used to hold the shipped product	100-P, 100-NP, 200-NC	Text	4	Internal list
Commodity Quantity	The number, amount, or count of the commodity being shipped	100-P, 100-NP, 200-NC	Numeric	8	

Shipping Remark	A text field describing information relevant to the shipment or product	100-NP	Text	75	Free-form text field; determine what this field contains, when used, etc.
Importer Signature	The importer's certification that forms were completed accurately	100-P, 100-NP, 200-NC	Text	35	Needs to be represented electronically
Importer Signature Date	The date on which the Importer Signature was applied	100-P, 100-NP, 200-NC	Date	8	
Service Official Name	The name of the employee who certifies the import transaction	100-P, 100-NP, 200-NC	Text	30	This may be converted to Employee Number later.
Service Official Signature	The employee's certification that forms were completed accurately	100-P, 100-NP, 200-NC	Text	35	Needs to be represented electronically
Service Official Signature Date	The date on which Service Official Signature was applied	100-P, 100-NP, 200-NC	Date	8	Format: MM/DD/YYYY

THOUGHT POINTS

Here are some points to note:

- The volume of data resulting from the harmonization process is smaller than the amount of raw data collected; this is a direct result of the harmonization process. Our raw data element listing contained sixty-one entries. Compare that to only twenty-one entries in our harmonized data element listing!

- When recording domain information, define the harmonized data element as text or alphanumeric if any single data digit contains an alphabetic character.

- When recording the length of the element, define the length of the harmonized data element as equal to the longest single raw data field.

- Develop data element definitions for the harmonized elements that are as succinct as possible but still consistent and complete. If it is a code, call it a code; if it's a date, call it a date.

- You may want to assign identifiers or reference numbers to each of the harmonized data elements. These don't have to be anything fancy; they simply constitute a way to identify and indicate specific data elements, particularly when your harmonized list is very large. This can be easily handled as a sequential numbering scheme, starting at 001 and incremented by one for each data element.

- Above, we only recorded each data element's name, definition, corresponding form, length, domain, and relevant comments. You may want to keep more metadata than this. For example, is a specific data element highly critical? Is a specific data element going to be eliminated in the near future?

- Later in the life cycle, you will associate the harmonized data elements to other objects, such as functional requirements, business process diagrams, or possibly, use cases.

I'll offer one last recommendation regarding naming the individual data elements: use representation terms. A representation term is used to express the category of a data element; it is generally the last word of the data element name. For example, the IJIS Institute recommends the following list of representation terms (plus others not listed):

- Amount

- Code

- DateTime

- Identifier

- Indicator

- Measure

- Quantity

- Text

SUMMARY

Using all the information gathered over the initial phases of our data analysis, you can begin the in-depth data analysis and harmonization. Start harmonizing the data by tackling the data elements that are obviously similar and represent the same pieces of data. Next, move on to the more abstract concepts. Remember to include details about qualifiers, metadata, and relationships, as that information will be critical later in the development life cycle.

One of the goals of harmonizing data is accounting for all the data that is required for stakeholders to make their decisions. The list of harmonized data elements will be fewer in number but more succinct in meaning and easier to work with when relating the data to business processes. Use the recognized representation terms when possible; this will allow for simpler integration and predictable results for folks outside the immediate project.

Chapter 6

Grouping the Data

Once you have a harmonized list of data elements, you'll want to start formulating ways to group the data elements into meaningful subject or functional areas based on some aspect or aspects of the client's business. This may require you to dig a little deeper into the business process side of the analysis to gain an understanding of points at which data is being entered, passed, or manipulated.

Remember the piles of forms, interview notes, data models, and website URLs that you gathered in the data collection phase of this process? Well, dig them out and dust them off because those artifacts will be the primary source of information to help you define the interaction between data and the business processes that manipulate that data.

I recommend starting this process of grouping the data elements by stepping back and analyzing the big picture. You don't want to dig too deeply into the client's business process; just get enough detail to serve your goal of identifying the required data. Below are a few questions you may want to ask at this stage.

DEFINE THE HIGH-LEVEL BUSINESS PROCESS

- What line of business is your client in? Whether your client is in retail, customer service, import/export, or entertainment, chances are you will be able to neatly and easily define their general, high-level line of business.

- Where does the business process begin? Your client's process has to start somewhere! A good area to examine is where your client initially receives the data that you're interested in managing. For example, if the client owns a gas station and the tanks are nearly empty, the "refill empty tank" business process is initiated by a sensor in the tank detecting a low volume of fuel and transmitting a signal to a receiver above ground that alerts the owner that he needs to replenish the gas supply.

- Where does the business process end? The corollary to the above, another good indicator of how data is being utilized, is to define the successful end state or what data triggers the end state. In our example above, our successful end state is a full tank of fuel delivered by the supplier and made available to the customers.

- Who are the general categories of actors in the business process? You must determine who in the process uses the data that you have been tasked with managing and harmonizing. Is there a delivery person involved? A clerk? An accountant? And which pieces of data are of interest to each of these actors?

- Does the data originate from outside the client? In some cases, external actors may actually trigger the business process you are trying to define the data for.

That's okay because you're only interested in what data is coming in, not the process itself.

> An *actor* can be a single person, a group of persons, another business entity, or even a computer system.

The most valuable resource you have in this task is your SME interview notes and existing documentation that you have collected. There are very few experts who can explain what they do without imparting a good dose of business process. Also, review the instructions that accompany the forms; these instructions may indicate a sequence that must be followed in submitting, reviewing, and approving the forms. If you need clarification on any of the processes or data, contact the relevant SMEs. When you contact the experts, you should be well versed in their data, processes, and nomenclature. You will score big points with your clients and gain much credibility by talking to them in their jargon. This makes them more comfortable and more at ease, which translates to them dispensing more valuable information to you. Last, make every effort not to ask questions that have already been asked and answered during previous interactions. If you do, your client may mistakenly think you weren't listening and become slightly annoyed.

Let's get back to our client, Monty, and his import business. You'll recall the list of harmonized data elements that we completed at the end of chapter 5. Well, now we want to group those data elements together logically for review and presentation. Monty's Import Service presents several different opportunities for meaningful groupings of data.

GROUPING DATA BY ACTOR

At the highest and simplest level, Monty's Import Service receives goods and products from exporters and clears those products to cross the border into the United States. Given this high-level business scenario, the most obvious grouping for Monty's Import Service is to group by actor. Using actors as our basis for grouping, we can start with the exporter of each product—after all, the product has to be exported before it can be imported! Let's review our full listing of harmonized data elements and determine which are related to the exporter.

A review of the data listing reveals that the following data elements are associated with each exporter:

Data Element	Description	Comments
Exporter Name	The registered name of the entity acting as exporter in the import transaction	
Exporter Location	The country of residence for the entity acting as exporter in the import transaction	Values are standard ISO Country Codes, for example: GRC = Greece.
Origin Country Code	A code that identifies the country where the product was produced, manufactured, grown, etc.	Values are standard ISO Country Codes, for example: GRC = Greece.
Departure Port Code	A code that uniquely identifies the foreign port from which the shipment departed	Values are identical to TSA listings.

Notice that Origin Country Code is included above. Just because a data element doesn't start with the word "exporter" doesn't mean it is not related to the exporter group. When creating the logical groups, you should review *all* the data elements to be certain you discern less obvious elements that logically belong to an identified group.

Once the product has left the foreign port and is in transit, we know, based on our business process, that there is a conveyance that is being used to transport the product from the foreign port to the United States. In this client's case, we know the conveyance is always a truck because Monty only deals with land borders. By reviewing our list of harmonized data elements, we quickly determine that we have information on the conveyances (Carrier Code), and we can conveniently fold in the data describing the commodities as well. This makes perfect sense because a conveyance would not leave the foreign port unless it contained some merchandise in its trailer.

The grouping of data related to conveyance and commodity may look something like this:

Data Element	Description	Comments
Carrier Code	A code that uniquely identifies the transporter of the goods	Valid codes for this element available on http://www.mis.com/cc.
Commodity Code	A code that uniquely identifies the product being imported	Internal list
Tariff Code	A code that classifies the commodity using the international tariff nomenclature	Source: Harmonized Tariff Schedule
Container Type Code	A code that identifies the type of enclosure used to hold the shipped product	Internal list
Commodity Quantity	The number, amount, or count of the commodity being shipped	
Shipping Remark	A text field describing information relevant to the shipment or product	Free-form text field; determine what this field contains, when used, etc.

What happens next in Monty's business process? The truck arrives at the US border, and a trustworthy Monty's Import Service employee is there to greet the import.

Of course, the importer is there as well, ready to receive the product and, presumably, deliver it to his distributor as soon as possible. In our harmonized data element listing, we have labeled employees

as service officials. The service officials only become part of the process when the product arrives at the border. By recognizing this obvious fact, we can easily group Monty's Import Service and the arrival data elements together.

The grouping of these data elements may look like this:

Data Element	Description	Comments
Arrival Date	The date on which the conveyance crosses the border into the United States	Format: MM/DD/YYYY
Arrival Number	An assigned number that identifies an import transaction	Sequential numbering scheme
Entry Port Code	A code that uniquely identifies the domestic port at which the shipment crosses into the United States	Values are identical to TSA listing.
Service Official Name	The name of the employee who certifies the import transaction	This may be converted to Employee Number later.
Service Official Signature	The employee's certification that forms were completed accurately	Needs to be represented electronically
Service Official Signature Date	The date on which the Service Official Signature was applied	

The last activity in this business process is the importer taking ownership of the merchandise after the Monty's official signs off on it. Since we have so diligently named our data elements, we know the harmonized data elements describing the importer are actually prefixed with the word "importer." What could be easier? Man, are we good or what? The last logical grouping of data is below:

Data Element	Description	Comments
I m p o r t e r Name	The registered name of the entity acting as importer in the import transaction	
I m p o r t e r Address	The physical address of the entity acting as importer in the import transaction	Includes street, city, state and postal code
Importer Code	The code that uniquely identifies an importer	SME Interviews; valid codes for this element in table IMPORTER_ CDS
I m p o r t e r Signature	The importer's certification that forms were completed accurately	Needs to be represented electronically
I m p o r t e r Signature Date	The date on which the Importer Signature was applied	

BENEFITS OF GROUPING THE DATA

Let's examine the advantages of logically grouping the data elements together:

- Divide and conquer: By grouping the data elements into logical areas, the different actors can review the data that pertains only to them. Of course, the other data would be available as well, but the various actors won't need to sift through pages of peripheral data and information to verify the portions of the data that deal with their particular areas of expertise.

- Completeness: When grouping data together in this manner, you may be able to identify data that needs to be available but that has not yet been discovered through your analysis up to this point. For example, maybe Monty's Import Service needs to record the license plate of each truck as a secondary identifier.

This data element would logically fit in the arrival grouping above.

- Gap analysis: Identifying loners and orphans is an ongoing process. After dividing your complete listing of data elements into logical groupings corresponding to the actors in the business process, review to ensure that all the elements have been assigned to a group. If you have a data element in the main list that has not been assigned to a group, do you really need that data? Review your analysis and identify why this data element was recorded in the first place and by whom.

- Data sharing: If a particular data element logically falls into more than one grouping, that is perfectly acceptable. In fact, this information is valuable to you and your client because they will understand that they are not operating in a vacuum concerning data and their actions can impact seemingly unrelated business areas.

GROUPING BY PROCESS

Normally, there will be many ways to group the data. A second suggestion for this exercise is to dissect the import process itself, separating it into its elementary components. In this scenario, we may group data by the following processes:

- Export: departure from foreign location

- En route: in transit from departure location to destination location

- Arrival: reaching the US border

- Review and approval: Monty's Import Service approval of the delivery

- Receipt: importer taking ownership of the imported product

Once you have completed grouping your data, you can create reports in your data management tool to reflect all the logical groupings that you have developed. Each of these reports can then be stored and retrieved as needed, depending on the situation. For example, you may have a report called Group By Actor and another called Group By Action. Another suggestion is to create other reports that are sorted based on one or more of the attributes you've defined (the metadata). For example, create a report sorted by length of data element or sort the data by criticality to the project. A very simple and straightforward (and very helpful) report is one simply sorted alphabetically by data element name.

The tool you are using should have the capability to create graphics based on the data listings and metadata; presenting the groupings graphically is a wonderful method for very clearly communicating your analysis. Your diagram could be something as simple as this:

This diagram clearly illustrates the breakpoints in the process. You may choose to note the data elements that are relevant to each module of the process in this diagram as well. For example, associate all the exporter data elements with the departure business process module. This not only clearly illustrates the association between the business process and the data but also provides a more complete and comprehensive view of the analysis. Ensure the process diagrams, even at a high level, start at the inception and progress to completion.

We'll discuss the topic of presentation at length in chapter 8.

SUMMARY

There are many ways to slice, dice, and group the data you've recorded up to this point; find the presentation method that resonates best with your client. After all, your goal is to clearly communicate data requirements to your client! In this chapter, we grouped our data elements by actor in the first example and by business process in the second example. There are plenty of other subject and functional areas that can be utilized to segregate data into subject matter that your client will easily understand.

A benefit of grouping and sorting your data elements is ease of presentation; each area can be presented to only those individuals who are relevant to that particular area. You will also easily identify data that is shared across project or program boundaries. Grouping and sorting will also allow you to identify gaps in your analysis and recognize areas where more data may need to be captured.

Chapter 7

Practical Applications of Data Analysis

Up to this point, we have been using Monty's Import Service and the actors involved in the import process as the main example in this book. Monty's provides us with a relatively easy business model to follow and a limited set of data to analyze, and it presents opportunities to practically apply the concepts that I am presenting in this book. But data harmonization is applicable to many other industries.

I would like to take this opportunity to recall a few occasions where the principles discussed in this book were used to consolidate and streamline the inefficient storage of data.

Managing the Inventory

Many moons ago, I worked for an organization that maintained the inventory of parts used in the construction and maintenance of automobiles. The inventory strategy and storage approach were based on the four general categories of parts related to a vehicle: the interior, the exterior, the engine, and the wheels. At first glance, this seems like a very practical, straightforward, and logical way to organize the inventory (and data). But the company was experiencing situations where parts were categorized incorrectly, the amounts and totals appearing on reports were inaccurate, and external customers who placed orders were receiving the wrong parts. These are serious issues! When we were called in to help, we discovered some ripe opportunities for harmonizing the data.

As we discussed in previous chapters, the process starts by gathering all the sources of data. In this case, the parts inventory was kept in four systems; each corresponding to the four different categories of parts. Below is an abbreviated listing of the contents of each system:

Interior	Exterior	Engine	Wheels
I-1223 Brake Pedal	E-3113 Trunk Latch	E-5233 Cylinder	W-7226 Gold Rims
I-1443 Leather Seat	E-3787 Rims	E-5245 Timing Chain	W-7549 Lug Nuts
I-1444 Vinyl Seat	E-3758 Head Lamp	E-5119 Fuel Injector	W-7622 Chrome Rims
I-1889 Odometer	E-3788 Sun Roof	E-5298 Dip Stick	W-7409 Hub Cap
I-1768 Dash Board	E-3871 Bumper	E-5293 Turbo	W-7928 Tire
I-1665 Moon Roof	E-3872 Bump Guard	E-5294 Turbo Extra	W-7879 Extra Wide
I-1145 Gear Shift	E-3875 Grill Guard	E-5489 Air Filter	W-7213 Black Rims

Obviously, there were many more parts listed in the inventories of each of these areas, but for the purposes of our discussion, we can settle on this limited crosscut of data.

Okay, let's say that you and I have been hired by this client to streamline, consolidate, and reorganize their data stores to realize more efficiency and accuracy in their data storage, retrieval, and reporting. As we review the documentation available to us, we can begin to formulate a plan to harmonize the inventory data by reducing the volume of data being stored, eliminating the redundancy that we discover in the data, and constructing a more reliable and accurate data storage strategy.

As we dig deeper into the documentation, we discover that each system contains more or less the same data elements—much more than simply the part number and the part name. In fact, let's list all the data fields in each of the systems and look for the low-hanging fruit! Remember, we performed the same analysis on Monty's, but we took the data elements from the forms instead of from the systems. Same concept, different industry! Here is a listing of the current system fields:

Interior	Exterior	Engine	Wheels
Part Number	Part Num	Part No	Part Identifier
System Indicator	System Code	Int_Ext	Short Description
Short Description	Short Desc	Eng_Whl	Long Description
Long Description	Long Desc	Short Part Text	System Type
Color Code	Color	Long Part Text	Wheel Type
Current Amount	Reorder Amt	Material	Current Amount
Reorder Amount	Current Amt	Current Amt	Reorder Amount
Last Update Date		Reorder Amt	Last Update Date
			Last Update User

Our first task is to begin constructing our basic cut of the harmonized data set. Since all the systems are composed of basically the same record structure, let's start at the top with the identifier of the part. Each system has its own unique label for a part: it's labeled Part Number in the Interior system, Part Num in the Exterior system, Part No in the Engine area, and finally Part Identifier in the Wheels system. As we did with Monty's, let's define these data elements, discover the similarities, and start to harmonize the data.

By reviewing the current system documentation and interviewing the SMEs, we compile the following table for the first field in the record, Part.

Data Element	Description	Domain	Comments
Part Number	A number that uniquely identifies a part	Alpha	Format: X-NNNN, where X is a letter and NNNN is a four-digit number
Part Num	A number that identifies a part in inventory	Alpha	
Part No	An indicator describing a unique part being stored in inventory	Alpha	
Part Identifier	A sequence of letters and numbers that uniquely identifies a part used in the construction of a vehicle	Alpha	

Since all the definitions for a part are basically the same, we can create one data element, called Part Number, that will store the designated data element and its metadata. By doing so, we can encompass all four of the systems' part labels in a single field. To take this example a step further, we can consider consolidating all four schemas of Interior, Exterior, Engine, and Wheels into one large schema that consists of all the harmonized inventory data elements. This eliminates the same data element, Part Number, being held redundantly in four different systems but actually representing the same data. In other words, it doesn't matter that a part has been labeled as an "exterior part," the fact that the object *is* a part of any system inventory and identified by a unique part number makes it an identifiable object in the harmonized data structure. Next, let's analyze the data that designates the inventory system to which a specific part belongs.

Again, let's list them out and define the data in the same manner we did for Part Number:

Data Element	Description	Domain	Comments
System Indicator	An indicator of the system	Alpha	Valid values: I, E, E, W
System Code	A code that designates the area where the part is stored	Alpha	Valid values: I, E, E, W
Ing_Ext	An indicator of whether the part is for the interior or the exterior	Alpha	Valid values: I, E
Eng_Whl	An indicator of whether the part is for the engine or the wheel	Alpha	Valid values: E, W
System Type	A value indicating which system the part belongs to	Alpha	Valid values: I, E, E, W, A

There are several anomalies that we should recognize right off the bat:

- There are only four systems in this organization, and we have documented five occurrences of the system indicator in the comments column: I, E, E, W, and A.

- Even though all these data elements represent the same data, in the Engine system, the system indicator has been further defined using two data elements: Int_Ext and Eng_Whl.

- Last, there is a value (A) under the system type that is not represented in any of the other three elements.

Being the crack data analysts that we are, we set off to find some answers to explain these anomalies. We interview the SME and the system administrator and quickly ascertain that the further delineation of the System Indicator in the Engine system was an effort to classify engine parts to a lower level of granularity than existed at the time. Our SME also mentioned that the concept is outdated and can be discarded. That will allow us to fold the data elements Int_Ext and Eng_Whl into the single harmonized data element called System Indicator. Nice work!

Okay, now let's investigate the item associated with the System Type. That would be the valid value of "A" available in the Wheels system. What does it represent? Is it still used? Should the value apply to the other three systems? These are all questions we'll pose to our SME. (Remember, your SME is the expert; leverage his expertise to solve any and all of the data issues.)

After the SME interview, we discover that A stands for "Add On," an old system component that was used to track items, such as pin-striping and spoilers, that were considered extras to the main construction process. The SME informs us that the Add On portion of the system was deprecated years ago and the parts that were designated as such were incorporated into the Exterior system. Unfortunately no one went back into the system and retroactively cleaned up the orphan values. So, in the final analysis, we'll remove A as a valid value for the harmonized element System Indicator in the new data set.

We will continue the review and analysis of the data, and eventually we'll construct our draft harmonized data set.

Data Element	Description	Length	Domain	Comments
Part Number	A number the uniquely identifies a part in inventory	5	Alpha	Format: X-NNNN, where X is a letter and NNNN is a four-digit number
System Indicator	An indicator designating the area of inventory where the part is stored	1	Alpha	Valid values: I, E, E, W

Short Description	An abbreviated textual description of the part	20	Text	Values should come from reference tables to be determined.
Long Description	An extended textual description of the part	100	Text	This field is free-form entry.
Color Code	A code indicating the color of the part	1	Alpha	Values should come from reference tables to be determined.
Current Amount	The physical count of a part in inventory	4	Numeric	
Reorder Amount	The physical count at which the supply of the part must be replenished	4	Numeric	An e-mail notification is generated to the steward of the system.
Material Code	The actual substance that composes the part	1	Alpha	Only used for parts designated as engine parts

Some important items to notice about the draft harmonized data set:

- The HDS is eight data elements. The original combined four systems stored over 30 data elements. Remember, the volume of data resulting from the harmonization process is generally less than the volume of the collective raw data.

- We have not included the attributes of Last Update Date and Last Update User. These elements are referred to as design attributes, which means they'll become part of the physical implementation of the HDS and will be used for audit trail purposes. Because these data elements will be included in every table, they generally are not harmonized.

- The Material Code is an orphan; it is only applicable to parts that are included in the construction of the engine. It is very important to note this fact for future reference. At the very least, if there is a listing of all the acceptable materials, we'll want to note that in the comments and verify the values.

- Last, notice that the System Indicator has the same value representing both Exterior and Engine, specifically the letter E. This is a problem that we'll need to bring to the attention of the reviewers when we present our artifacts. The work-around for this organization was identifying an Exterior part by using the prefix E-3 and identifying an Engine part by using the prefix E-5. (Refer back to the original listing of parts.) This needs to be cleaned up so the distinction is clear.

There is one last item to address: the redundancy in the data values themselves. If we review just the partial listing of inventory from earlier in the chapter, we can identify several data elements for which the value is ambiguous or flat-out redundant. I have circled the potential problem values.

Interior	Exterior	Engine	Wheels
I-1223 Brake Pedal	E-3113 Trunk Latch	E-5233 Cylinder	W-7226 Gold Rims
I-1443 Leather Seat	E-3787 Rims	E-5245 Timing Chain	W-7549 Lug Nuts
I-1444 Vinyl Seat	E-3758 Head Lamp	E-5119 Fuel Injector	W-7622 Chrome Rims
I-1889 Odometer	E-3788 Sun Roof	E-5298 Dip Stick	W-7409 Hub Cap
I-1768 Dash Board	E-3871 Bumper	E-5293 Turbo	W-7928 Tire
I-1665 Moon Roof	E-3872 Bump Guard	E-5294 Turbo Extra	W-7879 Extra Wide
I-1145 Gear Shift	E-3875 Grill Guard	E-5489 Air Filter	W-7213 Black Rims

As you can see, this organization has four different references to a part labeled rims in two different systems. No wonder the numbers on their reports were wrong! Also, notice that in the Interior system, there is a part called I-1665 Moon Roof, and in the Exterior system, there is a part called E-3788 Sun Roof. Are these actually the same part? Obviously, there is still some work to be done. Don't worry; we will discuss data value consolidation at length in chapter 9.

To ensure that the whole process is clear, let's review one more scenario that demonstrates the principles of data harmonization. Again, I will draw on one of my past assignments. I worked with an agency that prided itself on educating its employees. It was a firm believer in expanding the expertise of all the employees— from the administrative staff all the way up to the CIO. As noble as this idea was, the agency had a problem with tracking the training courses that employees planned to attend as well as the trainings that the employees had already completed. Questions started to arise: Which employees had taken which courses? Were the bills for various classes already paid? Or worse, had they been paid twice?

Let's imagine that, due to our collective expertise in data analysis and harmonization, you and I have been hired by this client to streamline, consolidate, and reorganize their data to increase the efficiency, accuracy, and reliability of the data being processed and reported. Let's get to work!

As our first step, we'll again begin by gathering our sources of data. This agency has two departments that are responsible for collecting and maintaining education and training courses for the employees. The first department deals mainly with the technically oriented training for the software developers, database administrators, and other technical staff. The training data is recorded in a spreadsheet that is stored on a common shared drive, and responsibility for keeping the data updated is shared among several employees who have access to and maintain the system. Below is a snapshot of the spreadsheet for the technical staff that we've obtained in the initial round of data gathering.

Emp Id	Dept	Course Id	Course Nm	Start Dt	End Dt	Location	Comp
T71207	DMG	D-100	Intro to Data	12/1/08	12/3/08	US	Y
T71207	DMG	D-200	Inter Data	1/3/09	1/7/09	US	Y
T20039	DWG	W-101	Intro to DW	2/8/09	2/10/09	CA	Y
T28551	EDA	EA1000	EA Basics	10/17/09	10/20/09	US	Y

The second department is in charge of maintaining the training information for the administrative side of the organization. The employees in these positions include project managers, business analysts, and technical writers. The training information is recorded and maintained on a spreadsheet as well but is stored on a different network drive and maintained by a separate group of employees. Below is a snapshot of the spreadsheet for the administrative employees, also acquired in the initial round of data gathering.

Employee Name		Vendor	Subject Area	Start Dt	Duration	Cert?
Benson	Ben	Train All	PMP Boot Camp	4/18/10	5	Yes
Sweet	Melissa	Learn It Now!	Intro to Contracts	6/20/10	3	No
Mann	Luke	Learn It Now!	Get New Business	7/25/10	2	No
Volkov	Nick	Know It All	Time Management	9/4/10	1	No

We discover some additional information during our analysis and interviews:

- The organization as a whole has a preferred group of vendors to provide training for the employees.

- Each employee has one and only one unique employee identifier.

- The cost of the individual course is dependent upon the number of employees attending the course: the greater the number of employees attending, the less the course will cost for each attendee. Notice that cost of the training course is not captured in the spreadsheet; this may be a problem.

- An employee makes a request for training by simply sending an e-mail to one of the coordinators in the education group; the e-mail is to include as much pertinent information about the course or topic as the potential student knows at the time of the request.

- Last, when an employee attends a training course, that employee is expected to complete the course successfully.

Our first task is to list all the data elements of interest to the organization as a whole and look for opportunities to harmonize. Here is a listing of the data elements with associated metadata (by now, this should look pretty familiar):

Data Element	Description	Length	Domain	Comments
Employee Id	A number that uniquely identifies an employee	6	Alpha	Format: XNNNNN X = T (technical employee) or A (admin employee) NNNNN = generated number
Department Code	An indicator designating the department where the employee works	3	Alpha	Valid values are found in table DEPT_CD.
Course Id	A number that uniquely identifies a training course	5	Text	
Course Name	A textual description of the training course	20	Text	
Start Date	The date on which the training course begins	8	Date	Format: MM/DD/YYYY
End Date	The date on which the training course ends	8	Date	Format: MM/DD/YYYY
Location	A code designating the country in which the training took place	2	Alpha	Valid values are found in table CNTRY_CD.
Complete	A code indicating if the employee finished the course	1	Alpha	Valid Values: Y and N
Employee F Name	The first name of the employee	50	Alpha	
Employee L Name	The last name of the employee	50	Alpha	
Vendor Name	The name of the company that offers/provides training	50	Alpha	Preferred vendors: Train All, Learn It Now!, and Know It All

Subject Area	The functional area covered by the training course	50	Alpha	
Start Date	The date on which the training course begins	8	Date	Format: MM-DD-YYYY
Duration	The number of days the training course will last	2	Numeric	
Certification Indicator	A code indicating if the course contributes to a certification	1	Alpha	Valid Values: Y and N

Now that we have all the data elements laid out in front of us, let's analyze the data and start harmonizing! Do you see any obvious redundancy? I do! Let's start with the data elements pertaining to the time period and duration. Those data elements are extracted and shown below:

Data Element	Description	Length	Domain	Comments
Start Date	The date on which the training course begins	8	Date	Format: MM/DD/YYYY
End Date	The date on which the training course ends	8	Date	Format: MM/DD/YYYY
Start Date	The date on which the training course begins	8	Date	Format: MM-DD-YYYY
Duration	The number of days the training course will last	2	Numeric	

Extracting a subset of the data from the main data set listing clearly illustrates the redundancy we seek to remove. We have two data elements (one from each system) that describe exactly the same data, namely, the start date. We can immediately eliminate one data element. The next issue on our plate concerns the duration of the course versus the end date of the course. We, as data analysts, will recommend not keeping both an element representing end date and an element representing duration. Here's why: If we have the start and end date, we can easily determine the duration of the training course. Conversely, if we have the start date and the duration, we can easily determine the end date of the course. Given this information, we shall keep a start date and an end date as part of the HDS.

Next, let's examine the data element labeled Complete in conjunction with the interview notes. The Complete data element is defined as an indicator of whether the employee completed the course or not. When we interviewed the SME, he stated that when an employee attends a training course, that employee is expected to complete the course. If this is truly the case, then there is no need to record whether an employee finished the training course or not; the answer will always be yes. For this reason, the data element Complete can safely be eliminated from the harmonized data set we are compiling.

We will continue to analyze and harmonize until we have reached a point where our first cut of the HDS is complete. Below is our draft HDS for this organization:

Data Element	Description	Length	Domain	Comments
Employee Id	A number that uniquely identifies an employee	6	Alpha	Format: XNNNNN X = T (technical employee) or A (admin employee) NNNNN = generated number

Employee First Name	The first name of the employee	50	Alpha	
Employee Last Name	The last name of the employee	50	Alpha	
Department Code	An indicator designating the department where the employee works	3	Alpha	Valid values are found in table DEPT_CD.
Course Id	A number that uniquely identifies a training course	5	Text	
Course Name	A textual description of the training course	20	Text	
Subject Area	The functional area covered by the training course	50	Alpha	
Vendor Name	The name of the company that offers/ provides training	50	Alpha	Preferred vendors: Train All, Learn It Now!, and Know It All
Start Date	The date on which the training course begins	8	Date	Format: MM/DD/ YYYY
End Date	The date on which the training course ends	8	Date	Format: MM/DD/ YYYY

Location Code	A code designating the country in which the training took place	2	Alpha	Valid values are found in table CNTRY_CD.
Course Fee	The fee charged for a specific training course	5.2	Numeric	Expressed in US dollars
Certification Indicator	A code indicating if the course contributes to a certification	1	Alpha	Valid Values: Y and N

You should note a couple of important issues regarding the draft harmonized data set:

- As we have seen in past examples, the volume of data resulting from the harmonization process is less than the volume of the collective raw data. In this particular case, the raw data had fifteen data elements, but the HDS has only thirteen.

- We have created a new data element called Course Fee to record the cost of the course. We created this new element because one of our client's main issues was recording and tracking training course costs.

In chapter 6, we discussed grouping our data set by actor for easier presentation to the client. In the scenario just analyzed, grouping by actor would be appropriate because there are really only two actors of interest: the employee and the training course. The following data elements are associated with the actor employee: Employee Id, Employee First Name, Employee Last Name, and Department Code. The remainder of the HDS can be grouped with actor Training Course.

Summary

The principles of data analysis and harmonization can be practically applied to many different industries. By describing different organizations and their array of data storage and maintenance problems, you can easily see that "bad" data can be the beginning of other problems and adversely affect business processes, data accuracy, data reliability, and even the financial bottom line.

Now it's time to return to our old friend and client, Monty's Import Service. Let's discuss the all-important presentation of all that hard work!

CHAPTER 8

PRESENTING YOUR ANALYSIS

Now that you have completed some outstanding data analysis and harmonization, it's time to communicate your initial findings, artifacts, and work products to the client for their review and feedback. To say that this first presentation is important would be a gross understatement. This presentation stands at the same level of importance as the analysis itself. This is an opportunity for you to demonstrate to the client that you understand their business, that your solution will make a difference in how their business operates (that is, add value), and that the financial resources they have invested in you were resources well-spent. As with the analysis itself, preparation is the key to a successful presentation!

The first task in effectively presenting your material is to get the right people in the room. There is very little business value for your client if you are presenting all this great work to individuals who had nothing to do with the project.

If possible, invite representatives from all the organizational entities involved in the interviews and analysis. In the same vein, invite a crosscut of

the organizations, including responsible persons from all aspects of the operations, to attend the meeting. In other words, the more layers of the organization that are represented, the more constructive the whole presentation will be. If possible, invite the CIO, mid-level managers, and end users. The more executive-level members of the organization that you can physically get into the meeting room, the better. Getting buy-in from the executive level is extremely important. If the leadership of the company doesn't agree with your analysis, you'll have a more difficult time convincing the folks under them that your ideas are the right ideas. If a person was interviewed during the analysis process, you are obligated to invite that person to the meeting. Whether or not that person accepts your invitation is up to him or her.

Once you have determined who will be attending the presentation, it's time to confirm a time and location. This seems like a no-brainer, but when you're dealing with an array of personnel from multiple levels of the organization, this task can take on a life of its own. The priority at this stage of the preparation is to schedule sufficient time to completely present the materials, elicit meaningful discussion, and garner important feedback and comments from your client. A second priority at this point is to ensure that you respect your client's time.

Obviously, the invitees have other responsibilities; make effective use of their time and ensure the physical location is easily accessible! If you're having difficulty determining the amount of time needed for the meeting, review other project presentations of the same magnitude and use them as a point of reference for duration. Discuss the time allotment with others in your organization and the client organization to define a duration that will both respect your client's busy schedule and still allow ample time to garner all the feedback necessary to ensure an improved work product.

A few days prior to the actual meeting, send out the meeting materials to the expected attendees for their review. Make sure all the slides are in color and a legend is provided when appropriate. Accompany the slides with a paragraph or two explaining what the materials are and your reason for sending them. This serves several purposes: it allows the attendees the opportunity to thoroughly review the material beforehand (if they so choose), ask for any clarification of the materials, and formulate meaningful responses to any open issues identified in the presentation. Here's another really good reason for prior delivery of meeting materials: if an attendee unexpectedly cannot attend due to a schedule change, you have allowed them time to review and comment even though they will be physically unable to attend the meeting. In this manner, your client feels connected and involved; they'll have a voice even though they won't be present at the meeting.

PRESENTATION CHECKLIST

The day has finally arrived for you to present your analysis. Let's run through a checklist to help ensure the entire production goes off without a hitch!

- Always bring printed color copies of the presentation to the meeting. Bring as many copies as there are attendees. Many people will print their own copies prior to the meeting, but there will inevitably be a few folks who meant to but never got around to it. By making copies available, you won't lose meeting time while attendees leave briefly to print out their own copies.

- Always bring a soft copy of your presentation, whether that means bringing your laptop to the meeting or retaining a copy of the presentation on a flash drive or CD.

- If possible, bring your own projector (and projector bulb) to the meeting.

  Even if your client proudly states that all the audiovisual requirements are accounted for, bring the projector anyway; you will forgo the embarrassment of not being fully prepared to deliver your presentation. You will lose valuable credibility with your client if they view you as unprepared for the meeting. Take a page from the Boy Scout manual and be prepared!

- Check with the point of contact (POC) to determine if the conference room you'll be presenting in has a speakerphone that allows multiple people to phone in and participate via conference call. This is a great way to get even more people to participate and hear how great your solution is!

- Come early, stay late. By all means, be on time and stay on schedule! By arriving early, you can contact your POC, get to the conference room early, and make some critical decisions regarding seating, location of the electrical outlets, whether the built-in projector will be used, whether there are enough seats, and so on. Also, by arriving early and/or staying late, you may be able to elicit some extra information in a more relaxed atmosphere, instead of the rigid confines of the meeting. This is an ideal time to chat up the client and ascertain where you really stand at this point.

- Create material that will demonstrate to your client that you are aware of not only the solution to be presented but also the project management-related items of the task. To that end, you should have supplementary slides that cover such topics as:

- Meeting agenda: The agenda should state what material will be reviewed, the order in which it will be reviewed, and the manner in which the meeting will conclude.

- Task description: Include a sentence or two describing the task for which you were hired. This can be verbatim out of the SOW or a synopsis garnered from the aforementioned document. Either way, the description will provide convenient background for those who are not as familiar with the project and project goals.

- Assumptions: By identifying assumptions, you help set the scope of the project, assist in managing customer expectations, and define constraints that you're operating under to develop the work products.

- Accomplishments: Itemize what has been completed up to this point. Include a description of the task and a high-level description of the analysis and additional work that were performed as a precursor to this meeting.

- Timeline: Your timeline will reassure your client that you are operating within the time constraints of the contract, presenting timely artifacts, and not overutilizing resources and budget.

- Budget: If applicable, you may want to present any financial items that you feel should be highlighted. For example, if you've been very diligent about staying within budget, you may want to point that out to the client. This illustrates that you're spending their funds wisely and competently operating within the financial constraints set forth in the contract.

WRITE IT DOWN: GATHERING FEEDBACK

By now, you have completed the introductory materials and background portion of the presentation and moved full-force into the real meat and potatoes of the presentation: your data analysis and harmonization. There is one last thing I recommend that you do at this point—thicken your skin.

As you're presenting your hard work and analysis, you will have a variety of attendees who will be listening, digesting, analyzing, and, yes, criticizing your work. You should be very proud of the analysis you have performed up to this point. You should feel confident that the artifacts being presented are the best work you could accomplish given the task, constraints, assumptions, resources, and information at hand. But regardless of the quality of work, you may have a few folks in the room that will never be satisfied with your output and will always find fault with the analysis you're presenting.

Here's my advice to you in dealing with critics and cynics: First, don't take it personally; it is professional criticism. And second, listen to what they are saying. In fact, record everything that is discussed during your presentation.

A few years ago, I was working on a project that collected applications for financial assistance (generally referred to as welfare assistance). I had done a huge amount of data analysis, and I was finally ready to present the first draft of completed data artifacts to my client. I proudly displayed the first slide and declared confidently that we would be capturing the applicant's full name: first name, middle name, and last name. I started to move on to the next set of data but was rudely interrupted by one client who was less than ecstatic that I had been analyzing "his" data.

"Where are the aliases?" he asked.

"We aren't capturing alias names on the current form," I answered, quite sure of myself.

"I specifically asked for each applicant to have up to five aliases associated to them. We get alias names all the time! How am I supposed to keep track of these people if all they give me is an alias name?" It was obvious this gentleman was feeling like his voice had not been heard during the initial focus sessions.

At that point, I took some actions to diffuse a potentially combative atmosphere. I graciously thanked him for bringing this information to my attention, and I let him know that I would immediately make note of the change in the data requirements. I also mentioned that I would review the meeting minutes from that particular meeting and ensure they were complete and accurate and that any oversights pertaining to this data would be corrected as soon as they were identified. And guess what? I had just gotten an extremely important data requirement that was instrumental to the success of the client's business process: every name could have up to five aliases associated with it. (And, by the way, I did check the meeting minutes from our previous meeting, and there was no mention of alias names!)

In these presentations, capture as much detail as possible; after all, your client is the expert and is also funding your efforts.

They will have definite ideas regarding their expectations and what they desire to see from your efforts. Here are a few more recommendations to keep in mind for effective recording of the proceedings:

- Who made the comment: Always, always, always capture who in the room (or on the phone) made a comment, recommendation, or statement. This is very important because the source of the comments can give you insight as to who is listening, who actually cares about the material, and what level in the organization is most invested.

- Relevance: Always relate the comments made during the presentation to the relevant data item, artifact, or work product. There is nothing more frustrating to you or your client than when you've recorded feedback and are unable to relate it to something specific or specifically presented.

- Get it right: Immense effort should be put into *not* contacting the client post-meeting to ask for information that he or she has already provided during the meeting. You'll lose credibility!

- Build consensus: Ensure that everyone in the meeting agrees on the changes that are requested. If there is a difference of opinion regarding the updates, make a concerted effort to find common ground and gain consent from all involved.

- Thank you: Another no-brainer, but, just take it as a friendly reminder. Don't forget to thank your client for their time, comments, and expertise.

You will be recording a lot of information at the review session. At this time, don't be concerned with the amount of information being taken in. The next steps in the process will allow you ample time to sift, sort, and review the volumes and determine which comments are constructive and will enhance the product and which comments were irrelevant and can be discarded or deferred.

Upon adjourning the meeting, assure the client that you welcome additional comments and feedback even after the review meeting has concluded. This allows them extra time to digest the material further and make any additional feedback known to you. One word of advice: announce a deadline for accepting post-meeting comments. You don't want feedback trickling in too long after you've finalized your analysis because scheduling constraints may not allow the comments to be included in the delivered artifact.

SUMMARY

Effectively presenting the analysis, artifacts, and works products to your client is one of the most important activities you will perform as a data analyst. You must take this responsibility very seriously. Make the effort to get the right people in the room at a location that is convenient for the client and ensure ample time to listen to and record the valuable feedback. Preparation is the key to success when executing the presentation!

Always bring both soft and hard copies of the presentation materials to the meeting and create additional slides to give the conference a solid context. Record everything mentioned in the meeting that is germane to enhancing the artifact in question. To this end, bring a second person with you to act as a scribe; this will ensure the accurate recording of ideas, comments, and feedback. Last, always allow your clients to contact you post-presentation to elaborate additional ideas.

CHAPTER 9

ANALYZE THE FEEDBACK

You have wrapped up a very successful presentation and review session and received rave reviews of your work products from the client! You have also received some excellent constructive criticism, comments, and ideas to improve the product even more (which you diligently recorded). Now it's time to analyze all these comments, feedback, and recommendations and incorporate them into your artifacts.

But, first things first—ensure an open line of communication with your client.

This entails sending them a note to thank them (yes, thank them again) for their time and valuable input. You should also lay out the schedule for the next phase of the process. Inform the client when you estimate you will complete the task of updating the data element list and suggest some tentative meeting times for review of the final product. This not only helps your planning but also assists your client in making

plans for the subsequent phases of the life cycle after the data analysis is complete and approved.

Now, you should get cracking on the comments, feedback, and recommendations that you received from the client. As you're reviewing and analyzing the feedback, realize that all comments and suggestions are not created equal. Some feedback is much more valuable and relevant to your work than other comments. I recommend creating a simple system of "weights" and assigning those weights to each comment. By doing so, you can rank each of the comments based on factors such as importance to the client, criticality to the end user, or software development priority. The weight or priority that is assigned to each data element will also need to be recorded. Generally, if a comment and the data it pertains to relate to the core business of the organization, then that particular comment will carry more importance (that is, carry more weight) than others. In terms of Monty's Import Service, this may mean assigning a higher priority to comments and data relating to the actual importation of the products versus the products themselves. After all, Monty's is conducting an import business! To store this attribute, we'll have to add metadata to our data management tool. We want to be able to relate each and every data element to the feedback that is associated to it and the criticality factor (or priority) assigned to it.

The manner in which you rank the comments doesn't need to be fancy or overly intricate; it just needs to serve the purpose at hand. Don't overcomplicate the process! By keeping it simple but meaningful, you add metadata that you can use later to clearly and easily communicate with your client and gain consensus on the changes that should be implemented. Plus, this gives you another way to present the data to your client. Below is a simple example of a metadata attribute to record priority:

Priority	An indicator of importance to the business	**High**: will immediately impact success of project; very visible; must be implemented **Medium**: will adversely impact success of project; will strengthen product **Low**: will minimally impact success of project; may be deferred

For example, your client may want to know how many of the suggested changes are ranked as high priority. When ranking the suggestions and recommendations, refer back to your notes for additional input and clarification. If your client stood up and shouted into a megaphone and pounded the table while making a suggestion, you may want to assign that suggestion a higher weight!

While reviewing and analyzing the feedback, be cognizant of areas that were mentioned an inordinate amount of the time as well as areas in which the client recommended a large number of changes. These are flags that may indicate you need to perform additional analysis or that you failed to identify required data elements in the initial analysis. This might be something as obvious as a missed form or file, or it could be an issue of identifying additional data elements that will be required to resolve the data fully. The SME interview notes will be a good resource to assist you and provide clarification in this area.

DO IT AGAIN: ADDITIONAL ANALYSIS AND HARMONIZATION

Just as you may need to add additional metadata to your list for clarification, you may also need to add new data elements or harmonize some of the existing data elements further. As I have mentioned several times, data harmonization is an iterative process.

Going back to our Monty's example, let's say that a mid-level manager in our review session stated that the company not only collects the port of departure and the port of entry but also has a business interest in recording any ports that the conveyance has visited en route to its final destination port (that is, the port of entry). This is an excellent discovery and exactly the type of information that we need in order to enhance our data analysis and present a better, more complete work product. Let's review what we have vis-à-vis port data:

Data Element	Description	Form	Domain	Length	Comments
Departure Port Code	A code that uniquely identifies the foreign port from which the shipment departed	100-P, 100-NP, 200-NC	Numeric	4	Values are identical to TSA listing.
Entry Port Code	A code that uniquely identifies the domestic port at which the shipment crosses into the United States	100-P, 100-NP, 200-NC	Numeric	4	Values are identical to TSA listing.

Our first inclination might be to simply add another data element to represent the port that is visited during the trip. But, upon reviewing the meeting minutes, we discover that a conveyance can visit multiple ports in the course of a single trip. Furthermore, there are many different reasons that a conveyance may make a stop at a port en route to its final destination. As it turns out, Monty's has a business interest in knowing the places the conveyance stops and why it is making each stop. Another great discovery!

So, our challenge is to represent the additional port or ports that are visited during the trip *and* to capture the reason for the port visits as well. Let's start piecing this puzzle together by taking a step back to review the data we already have.

1. We know that, using the Departure Port Code, we can identify the port where the trip began.

2. We also know the Entry Port Code can account for the port where the trip ended (in our case, the land border).

3. What do these two data elements have in common? They both represent a port. Upon deeper analysis, we realize that both data elements represent a port where some activity has taken place—this is a very important realization!

4. With this discovery, we can further harmonize Departure Port Code and Entry Port Code and just capture a single data element called Port Code.

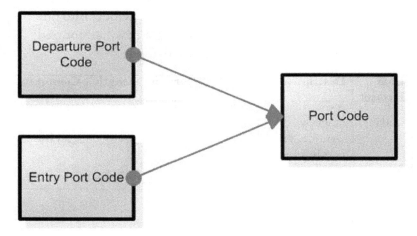

5. Now that we have a means of collecting the Port Codes involved in the trip, we now need to capture what activity or action transpired at the intermediate ports.

6. We can create a new data element called Port Activity Code, which can encompass and account for all actions that may occur at any port, not just the intermediate ports.

7. We will then relate the Port Code to the Port Activity Code that describes it. In data speak, the Port Code will be *qualified by* the Port Activity Code.

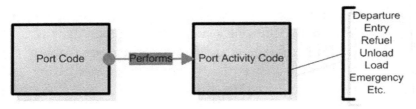

8. Now we can safely update our harmonized data element list by combining two existing data elements, Departure Port Code and Entry Port Code, into one new one (Port Code) and adding a new harmonized data element called Port Activity Code.

Data Element	Description	Form	Domain	Length	Comments
Port Code	A code that uniquely identifies the port involved in a shipping transaction	100-P, 100-NP, 200-NC	Numeric	4	Values are identical to TSA listing.

Port Activity Code	A code that uniquely identifies the action at a specified port	New	TBD	TBD	Must be related to a port; need to define metadata and valid values list.

With the obvious updates to the data element names, we have also updated some of the metadata as well:

- Notice that the definitions have changed to more clearly define the new and updated data elements.

- Under the Form column, we have simply listed the word "new" for the Port Activity Code. You may choose any method to describe new data elements, but make sure you can clearly identify them and are able to query them easily when the list is completed.

- The domain and the length have yet to be determined. Since this is a new data element, we'll need to review it with the client and get their input on what the codes should actually be and what they'll represent (and possibly new data storage requirements).

- Last, note that we have added comments reflecting that there is a dependency between Port Code and Port Activity Code. In other words, if a port code is identified as being part of a transaction, it must also have a reason (activity) identified as well.

VALIDATE THE ANALYSIS

To validate our harmonization process, let's test our new data structure. Let's run through a simple import business transaction and ensure that our data elements can be traced throughout the process and, more important, record the business data correctly.

1. A truck leaves the loading dock in Edmonton, Alberta:

- Port Code = Edmonton

- Port Activity Code = Departure

2. The truck stops at Calgary, Alberta, to refuel:

- Port Code = Calgary

- Port Activity Code = Refuel

3. The truck crosses the US border in Sherwood, North Dakota:

- Port Code = Sherwood

- Port Activity Code = Entry

By using this simple business scenario, we have validated our harmonization of multiple data elements representing port data into a single data element that is qualified by an activity code. This will ultimately make our data collection and storage much more efficient. Remember, our goal is to account for all the data required by the business to successfully complete its business process.

After completing the port data, let's review our findings and comments and search for other opportunities for harmonization. Again, we want to look back at our meeting minutes for clues to areas where data can be harmonized and more efficiently represented.

ANOTHER OPPORTUNITY FOR HARMONIZATION

In chapter 6 we analyzed the business process at a very high level in order to identify ways in which the data could be grouped and better communicated and presented. We discovered that grouping by actor was the best choice for Monty's Import Service.

Let's review the list of actors (and data elements) in Monty's transactional process:

- Exporter Name: the registered name of the entity acting as exporter in the import transaction

- Carrier Code: the unique identifier of the transporter of the goods

- Importer Name: the registered name of the entity acting as importer in the import transaction

Just as we did with the port codes, we again ask ourselves, what do these data elements have in common? They each represent an organization, agent, or entity. Upon deeper analysis, we realize that all the data elements represent an entity that is performing some role in the transaction process. By viewing the data in this manner, we could make a case for further harmonizing Exporter Name, Carrier Code, and Importer Code into a single data element called Entity. Then, as we did with the ports, we can qualify Entity with a role indicator to identify the function of that entity within the import transaction.

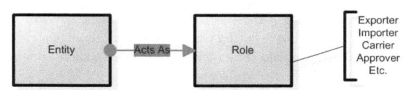

If we move forward with this harmonization, we'll need to update all the data elements involved, as well as create the new data elements required to account for and represent the data. We may use the port code harmonization as a template. Additionally, we'll need to test the new data structure by applying it to a simple business scenario to ensure we are capturing all the required data.

Once we reach a point in the data harmonization process where we're satisfied that the data element list is complete and succinct and that it clearly communicates the data requirements we're trying to capture, we need to review our budget and work breakdown structure (WBS) for the project to determine time and resource constraints. In other words, we need to decide which changes will be implemented. Do we have the budget to implement all changes? Should we concentrate on implementing only the changes that are identified as high priority? Do we have the resources to make the changes in the time frame outlined in the schedule? These are all questions that need to be discussed with the client before moving forward.

FINALIZE THE PRODUCT

At this point in the process, it's time to schedule a meeting to vet the changes from the initial presentation, gain approval, and deliver a fantastic finished work product. Refer back to chapter 8 for recommendations on establishing meeting logistics and protocol.

In this follow-up meeting, you want to ensure that what your client asked for was interpreted correctly. In other words, you don't want to hear, "That's what I said, but that's not what I meant." Be prepared to defend your changes, and by all means be ready to back up actions by pointing out who in the company suggested each change. Make clear that all the changes were based on suggestions, recommendations, and feedback garnered from the prior meeting or conversations with SMEs. You don't want to be accused of being a rogue data analyst!

SUMMARY

The feedback and comments you receive from the client should be thoroughly reviewed and analyzed with the goal of discovering ways to enhance and improve the final harmonized data set. All comments are not created equal, however, so developing a ranking system and assigning different weights to the comments will help you sift through the glut of feedback.

Just as you analyzed and harmonized the raw data set initially, at this stage you'll want to find opportunities for further harmonization of your data set. This may include harmonizing existing data elements for more clarity, creating additional data elements that will act as qualifiers, and even eliminating elements from the data set in some cases.

If you're unsure that a data element is appropriate or correct for your client's business process, test the data structure via a high-level business process scenario to ensure the data is suitable for the purpose it is intended. We performed our validation on the Port Activity Code to make certain we could account for all the activities that could take place at a particular port for a specific conveyance.

CHAPTER 10

ALMOST DONE: FINALIZE THE HDS

So, your meeting with the client was a great success! You vetted your proposed changes with the client and gained their approval to finalize all the changes and complete the harmonized data element listing. But before you launch headlong into finalizing the changes, there are some important tasks to complete:

- Audit trail: Ensure that the changes you are making are fully documented. That means recording who requested the change, why the change is being made and even who on your side completed the updates. This allows you to retain a history of the changes made to a particular element.

- Change management: Along the same lines of thinking, you must ensure that prior versions of the harmonized data element listing are available, stored, and retrievable. This is a secondary method of ensuring all changes are accounted for during the harmonization process; it also ensures that prior versions of the artifacts can be recovered and restored if necessary.

- Lineage: A key step in the harmonization process is capturing all the data elements that have been harmonized into a single element (plus a qualifier in some cases). This action allows you to maintain full traceability from the "as is" data elements to the harmonized data elements.

In the last chapter, we touched on the concept of having a data element that relies on another data element, the qualifier, to fully clarify the meaning of the data. In our example, the Port Activity Code was a qualifier of the Port Code; the two data elements are taken together to fully resolve the meaning of the data. The idea of two (or more) data elements being related or associated to one another is a structure that may or may not be familiar to your client. If the concept of a relationship between data elements is foreign to your client, you must thoroughly explain the linkage to them; otherwise, the harmonized data set will be difficult for them to understand.

Put in plain words, a relationship is "a quality that connects two or more things or parts as being or belonging or working together or as being of the same kind." In other words, both data elements can exist on their own, but taken as an ordered pair, they have a full, clear meaning in the context of the artifact. Again, ensure your client understands this concept!

An example that I have utilized many times to explain the use of a qualifier is a temperature reading. If someone asks what the temperature is and you respond by stating it is 57 degrees, would that be completely accurate? No, the person asking the question would be interested in knowing if it were 57 degrees Fahrenheit or 57 degrees Celsius; there is a big difference! By clarifying (or *qualifying*) the temperature, you can ascertain a complete picture of the situation and subsequently make a better, more informed decision.

Once all the updates have been completed, the audit trail is complete, and all the metadata has been entered, freeze the artifact. This means that no further changes or enhancements will be applied to the artifact—period.

The tool you are using to store the harmonized data set should allow you to take a baseline of the artifact and allow you to store it within the tool itself as well as to make a copy to store remotely at an offsite location.

It is now time to deliver the final artifact to your client. I recommend hand-delivering a bound hard copy of this work product if it's feasible. This not only assures that the right person has received and taken ownership of the work product, but it also gives you an opportunity to toot your horn regarding what a fine work product your amazingly talented team has produced. Additionally, if you are scheduled to deliver the product on a particular day and by a particular time, you want to ensure the deadline isn't missed due to the product sitting in the in box of the receptionist!

In addition to the personal delivery, you should plan to send the completed work product in soft copy form via e-mail to your client in both PDF and Word formats, plus any other format that the client dictates. Include all the persons necessary in the address list; don't rely on recipients to forward the artifacts to people on your behalf, because it may not happen. Don't hesitate to include an automatic response on the delivery e-mail, that way you know when the e-mail was opened and when the addressee presumably received and took ownership of the artifact.

Below is the final harmonized data element listing for Monty's Import Service (note that not all the metadata is included):

Data Element	Description	Form	Domain	Length	Comments
Arrival Date	The date on which the conveyance crosses the border into the United States	100-P, 100-NP, 200-NC	Date	8	Format: MM/DD/YYYY
Arrival Number	An assigned number that identifies an import transaction	100-P, 100-NP, 200-NC	Numeric	9	Sequential numbering scheme
Entity Role Code	A code that uniquely identifies the function in which the entity acted in a shipping transaction	New	Text	3	Valid values list is located on Monty's website under download section.
Entity Name	The registered name of the entity acting as a role in the shipping transaction	100-P, 100-NP, 200-NC	Text	30	Relationship to Entity Role Code; Entity encompasses Importer, Exporter, and Carrier.
Entity Address	The physical address of the entity acting as a role in the shipping transaction	100-P, 100-NP, 200-NC	Text	60	Includes street, city, state, and postal code
Importer Code	A code that uniquely identifies an importer	100-P, 100-NP, 200-NC	Alpha	9	SME Interviews; valid Codes for this element in table IMPORTER_CDS.

Carrier Code	A code that uniquely identifies the transporter of the goods	100-P, 100-NP, 200-NC	Alpha	5	Valid Codes for this element available on http://www. mis.com/cc.
Exporter Location	The country of residence for the entity acting as exporter in the shipping transaction	100-P, 100-NP, 200-NC	Text	3	Values are standard ISO Country Codes, for example: GRC = Greece.
Origin Country Code	A code that identifies the country where the product was produced, manufactured, grown, etc.	100-P, 100-NP, 200-NC	Text	3	Values are standard ISO Country Codes, for example: GRC = Greece.
Port Code	A code that uniquely identifies a port involved in a shipping transaction	100-P, 100-NP, 200-NC	Numeric	4	Values are identical to TSA listing.
Port Activity Code	A code that uniquely identifies the action at a specified port	New	Text	4	Must be related to a port; valid values list located on Monty's website under download section.
Commodity Code	A code that uniquely identifies the product being imported	100-P, 100-NP, 200-NC	Alpha	10	Internal list

Tariff Code	A code that classifies the commodity using the international tariff nomenclature	100-P, 100-NP, 200-NC	Numeric	10	Source: Harmonized Tariff Schedule
Container Type Code	A code that identifies type of enclosure used to hold the shipped product	100-P, 100-NP, 200-NC	Text	4	Internal list
Commodity Quantity	The number, amount, or count of the commodity being shipped	100-P, 100-NP, 200-NC	Numeric	8	
Shipping Remark	A text field describing information relevant to the shipment or product	100-NP	Text	75	Free-form text field; determine what this field contains, when used, etc.
Entity Signature	The certification that forms were completed accurately	100-P, 100-NP, 200-NC	Text	35	Needs to be represented electronically; Entity encompasses Importer, Exporter, and Carrier; relationship to Entity Role Code.
Entity Signature Date	The date on which the Entity Signature was applied	100-P, 100-NP, 200-NC	Date	8	Related to Entity Signature

Service Official Name	The name of the employee who certified the import transaction	100-P, 100-NP, 200-NC	Text	30	This may be converted to Employee Number later.
Service Official Signature	The employee's certification that forms were completed accurately	100-P, 100-NP, 200-NC	Text	35	Needs to be represented electronically
Service Official Signature Date	The date on which the Service Official Signature was applied	100-P, 100-NP, 200-NC	Date	8	Format: MM/DD/YYYY

THOUGHT POINTS

Below are some items to note upon review of the complete harmonized data set listing:

- The final artifact is much smaller than the original list and even smaller than the first draft of the data elements.

- The redundant data has been eliminated.

- Many individual data elements have been harmonized into a single representative data element.

- Unnecessary data elements have been eliminated.

- The data is represented in such a way as to be accurate and understood across the organizations and boundaries; the data is authoritative and of high quality.

DATA QUALITY

Back at the very beginning of this book, we discussed authoritative data and data quality. At this point, upon successful completion of our work product, let's revisit this concept and expand on it a bit. I explained that authoritative data is data that you provide and that is accepted by the consumer as reliable and accurate. The data you provide via the HDS is comprehensive, cohesive, and succinct. It has been vetted through the client and deemed understandable, accurate, and credible. There are many measurements of what constitutes "good" data; I prefer the data quality measurement dimensions created and used by Citizant, Inc.

The following table contains the seven dimensions of data quality along with a description and example. We have mentioned and discussed some of these already, but a few are new to our subject matter. Quality data consists of some or (preferably) all of these dimensions.

DQ Dimension	Description	Measure (Example)
Accuracy	Qualitative assessment to which data accurately reflects real-world object or matches original source of data	Percent of values that are correct when compared to actual value
Completeness	Degree to which values are present in the attributes that require them	Percent of data fields having values entered into them
Consistency	Degree to which redundant facts are equivalent across two or more databases	Percent of matching values across tables/files/records
Precision	Degree to which data is known to the right level of granularity	Percent of data fields having the appropriate level of granularity
Timeliness	Degree to which data is up-to-date and available to support a given knowledge worker or process	Percent of data available within a specified threshold timeframe
Uniqueness	Degree to which there are no redundant occurrences or records of the same object or event	Percent of records having unique primary key
Validity	Degree to which data conforms to its definition, domain values, and business rules	Percent of data having values that fall within their respective domain of values

Source: Citizant, Inc.

Ultimately, your goal is to effectively and clearly communicate your solution to the client and gain consensus among all the users of the data. The data harmonization process is the first step. In the case of Monty's Import Service, the three original forms are very close in content, and eventually we'll want to combine all three forms into one form that will handle the import regardless of commodity or location. That work can be accomplished in the next round of assigned tasks.

SUMMARY

As you are applying the final changes to the HDS, make certain you maintain a log of all changes to the artifacts and the reason for the changes. The audit trail continues to be a very important source of maintenance information. Discuss unfamiliar concepts with your client so they have a full understanding of the updates to the data element listing. Ideas such as relationships and qualifiers may be new to your client; make sure they understand them and fully comprehend how they were applied to the artifact.

The HDS should align with the data quality dimensions that we discussed and should be clear and easily communicated. The HDS should be frozen, baselined, and stored. The delivery of the final product should be completed on the date agreed upon by you and your client or stated in the SOW. The actual artifact should be delivered both in person and by e-mail. Provide the artifact in multiple formats, particularly any formats that your client requests and is comfortable with.

Chapter 11

Moving Forward After the HDS

Congratulations! You have completed the data harmonization for the client! Your client is now the proud owner of a comprehensive, standardized, harmonized listing of data elements that accounts for all the data they require in order to successfully complete their business processes. The harmonized data set represents the data that your client will be collecting, storing, manipulating, transmitting, and reporting in the organization's current system and, hopefully, in the target system as well.

Okay, we have this data element listing ... now what? Obviously, the next steps will be decided and driven by your client. But that doesn't mean you can't make a few suggestions. The fact that you have delivered a concise, comprehensive listing of data gives your client the foundation for creating additional artifacts and work products that will be valuable to the organization and move the client forward in the life

cycle. Some potential additional artifacts that you may want to provide, using the HDS as a foundation, include the following:

- Conceptual data model: A possible next step may be to create a conceptual data model. A conceptual data model is a high-level view of the organization's concepts and the relationships between those concepts. Constructing a conceptual model will allow you to begin the process of establishing relationships between the data elements of interest to the client and solidifying the functional areas identified. For example, in the case of Monty's Import Service, we documented that there is a carrier that utilizes a conveyance to transport a shipment that contains the product. The conceptual model for this scenario may look something like this:

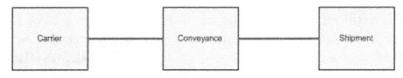

  Notice the conceptual model only uses a line to represent that two concepts or areas are related. You may choose to label each line to enhance the meanings of the relationship and put the concept into context. The conceptual model is just that—conceptual and purposefully high level.

- Logical data model: A logical data model is a method of representing an organization's data in an abstract structure that can be created using the data listing as a starting point. In the case of logical models, objects called entities represent the areas of interest, and the relationship between the entities is more descriptive than with the conceptual model. This model will further solidify (and communicate) the relationships between the areas and the data, as well as establish other properties of the data such as cardinality and optionality. We can revisit Monty's Import Service and enhance the conceptual model to create a logical model. The logical model for Monty's may look something like this:

Notice the additional information that is conveyed in the logical model versus the conceptual model. When modeling logically, the relationship line between the entities is always labeled to communicate a meaningful association between the entities. For example, a Carrier *utilizes* one or more Conveyance. Also, a Conveyance *transports* one or more Shipments. You can also indicate optional and mandatory relationships in the logical model as well. For example, a Conveyance *may transport zero, one, or many* Shipments; this relationship indicates that a conveyance may not transport any shipments (such is the case if the truck is empty), and thus the relationship is optional. The corollary of this relationship is mandatory: a Shipment *is transported by* a Conveyance. In other words, a shipment cannot ship itself; it *must* be transported by a conveyance. The logical model is another communication tool that you can use to pictorially represent the data requirements.

- Initial physical data model: Eventually, the data that we've defined and modeled will be implemented using data definition language (DDL) via a physical data model with database tables, referential integrity, and linkages. Think of the physical data model as the physical representation of the abstract logical model. Although this step is a little premature at this stage in the process, it certainly does no harm to start thinking about it. Again, using Monty's Import Service as our example, our physical model may be represented as follows:

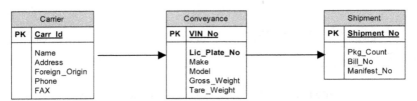

Notice that even more information is contained in the physical model versus the logical model. As we progress from conceptual to logical to physical, we continue to gain more clarity and functionality in the data requirements. You can see that each entity from the logical model is represented by a table in the physical model and contains additional data in the form of fields. For example, each record contained in the Carrier table will consist of Name, Address, Foreign_Origin, Phone, and Fax. Also, each record in the Carrier table will be uniquely identified by the field Carr_Id (or Carrier Identifier). Again, the physical model is very premature at this point, but it's helpful to see the possibilities that lie ahead.

- Enterprise architecture (EA): The HDS can provide a basis for the data layer of the EA framework. This data layer would be developed and architected in such a way that the data could be used as an enterprise shared service (ESS). As an ESS, the critical data becomes more centralized, allowing much easier access to the data and easier maintenance of the data asset. Creating a data layer that is accessible to all who need it is essential to eliminating the stovepipe mentality and framework.

CURRENT DATA AS A FOUNDATION FOR FUTURE ANALYSIS

The data will provide a solid stepping stone to get you to the potential next steps such as business process diagramming and, further along in the development process, other EA-, data- and process-related work products, such as business node connection diagrams, sequence models, and information exchange models.

My point is this: Do not allow all your hard work to end up as dust-gathering shelfware! Put it to good use and stress to your client that completion of this artifact represents the *beginning* of the next steps—not the end of the road.

To that end, start lobbying your client for more work. The next steps in the life cycle could be:

- In-depth analysis of the "as is" business processes, including detailed business process diagrams, with traceability to the data elements. Identify where in the business process specific data is collected, manipulated, and disseminated. We performed this operation at a high level when we grouped the Monty's Import data by process in chapter 6.

- Analysis of the current ("as is") work environment should yield target ("to be") business processes that are more streamlined and efficient and may lead to exploiting newer technologies or more effective integration with existing technologies. With Monty's stovepipe systems currently performing the same function in different locations, our recommended target environment would include implementing a single database shared among all three branch offices and eliminating the storage of redundant data elements.

- Extensive gap analysis identifying what changes need to be implemented in the business processes and what additional data elements may need to be captured in order to achieve the target state. In the case of the agency that prided itself on educating its employees, one glaring gap was the inability to effectively track costs. The recommended harmonized data set we created in chapter 7 accounted for that gap by including a data element that will store the fee for the training course. That agency may also want to integrate a history function that tracks both courses and payments.

- Compose a transition plan and a development plan to help steer the client's actions and solidify the scope of activities necessary to accomplish their business-process reengineering goals. For example, the inventory operation we discussed may want to include a detailed transition plan for integrating and consolidating their data stores. A development plan may include simplifying the user interface for the new target system functionality so all the employees have access to the required parts inventory.

- Creating the above artifacts will require in-depth focus sessions (sometimes referred to as deep dives) to accurately depict business processes and gather business rules that apply to both data and process activities. In our discussion of identifying data sources and gathering and reviewing the data artifacts, we elaborated on setting up interviews and focus sessions with the subject matter experts, as well as all interested stakeholders (within the constraints of the contract).

- A natural extension of the business process diagramming is the creation of use cases. A use case is a method of describing how the system will behave when an actor applies a business action. For example, when a user enters his user name and password, he will expect the system to present the main menu of the system. Use cases allow you to describe and communicate the target business processes in a way that is clearly and easily understood by people at all levels of expertise in the client audience. A use case usually consists of a title, a description of the functionality, a listing of the actors that may perform this function, and a series of numbered steps indicating the action performed by the actors and the expected behavior or results returned by the system.

- Another extremely useful artifact is a traceability matrix. Generally, once the functional requirements have been defined, a matrix can be produced to illustrate the association between the functional requirement and the test cases or the functional requirements and the data elements that support those requirements. You may choose to create a traceability matrix that lists the use cases and what functional and data requirements support those use cases. The possibilities are endless!

- Last, produce any work products that your client is willing to contract you to produce! You can suggest next steps and required artifacts, but it's really up to the client to drive the next tasks to be accomplished.

CHANGE CONTROL STRATEGY

As you begin associating the data to the business processes, you will encounter situations in which the data needs to change, new data elements need to be added, or some data elements need to be eliminated or harmonized. This is not a problem and is a natural progression of in-depth data and business analysis. But before you make any changes, you need to establish a change control strategy.

Just as we tracked changes in the HDS, we need to track and control changes to the data artifacts and to all artifacts that we'll be producing as well. A simple change control framework should be established to identify change requests that are submitted and how they will be resolved. A straightforward change-request cycle may consist of four states:

- Submitted: When a change is submitted, capture who made the submission, when it was actually submitted, and the area that would potentially be impacted by the change. Inform the requestor that the change was received and is in "submitted" status.

- Review: Establish a specific date and time that submitted changes will be reviewed. This may be based on a calendar day (for example, the first Tuesday of each month) or may be based on the number of submissions accumulated to trigger the review. Once again, inform the requestor that the change is in status "review."

- Decision: In order to keep the cycle as simple as possible, render only two decisions. The change is either approved or denied.

- If the request is denied, a good rule of thumb is to communicate the reason for the disapproval to the requestor and to indicate whom questions should be directed to regarding the decision.

- If the request is approved, communicate the estimated date on or by which the change will be implemented.

- Implementation: Once a change is implemented, capture the date on which it was implemented and any other pertinent materials and metadata; these will become part of your audit trail.

IMPLEMENT A DATA GOVERNANCE PLAN

One of the last concepts that I'll introduce and discuss is the implementation of a data governance program. Think about it: you have created a set of data that is standardized, harmonized, complete, and agreed upon. Any changes to the data or the processes that impact the stability of the data must be controlled and structured. This is the value of a well-planned, rigorous data governance program. Though a full discussion of data governance is beyond the scope of this book, you should research this topic to gain a thorough understanding of it. Generally speaking, data governance is creating and implementing standards that govern the collection, storage, and usage of data. These standards help to ensure the reliability and integrity of the data is not diminished when new data is introduced or new business processes are developed. It validates the data being captured (particularly unstructured data), verifies the integrity of the data that is collected, and assures that all data captured conforms to the policies and administrative standards implemented by your organization or by your client.

Data governance must also include maintenance of the metadata. The metadata will be tied closely to the physical database structures in the implemented process. The governance process should be flexible enough to allow for changes to the services that take in and distribute the data, while still maintaining a rigid set of standards so the existing data is not impacted or corrupted. Depending on the organization's size and maturity, your client may or may not have a data governance plan in place. If your client doesn't have a governance plan in place, this may become another opportunity for you to score additional work.

SUMMARY

The final approved data element listing is potentially the starting point and foundation for many other future development efforts. We mentioned several artifacts that can be built from the HDS, such as a conceptual data model and a logical data model. You may choose to progress the business process area and begin diagramming the current business processes and advancing to the future processing target state. The HDS will accurately bind these two artifacts together in a comprehensive manner. Further in the development cycle, you may choose to compose use cases and relate the business processes and the data to those use cases for a comprehensive picture of target system functionality.

As you move forward, suggest a change management strategy if your client does not already have a method in place. Utilize a simple process that everyone can agree on, that everyone understands, and that maintains the goal of tracking changes to the artifacts. In addition to change control, introduce the idea of implementing a data governance plan and framework. If your client already has an existing data governance plan in place, perhaps suggest a review of the plan to identify potential enhancements for the future.

CHAPTER 12

WRAP IT UP

Let's revisit that dreadful scenario that I described in the very first chapter. Remember that poor employee who was sweating bullets because he had to pull together all the data to produce the monthly report? Well, guess what? He has reviewed, analyzed, and harmonized the data required for the report and is no longer anxiety ridden at the very thought of compiling it. Once the data sources were analyzed, consolidated, and made easily accessible, the job is much easier to complete and takes much less time.

Let's recap just how we came up with an improved version of the existing data while more or less maintaining the same business process. The examples used in this book were fairly simple to allow you to understand how the concepts of data analysis and harmonization could be practically applied to a business situation. When you're hired to perform this task in the real world, however, the volume of data and the complexity of the relationships will most likely be much greater. The sheer enormity of the amount of data can feel overwhelming—but don't let it get to you! Remember what I recommended in the preface: start at the beginning!

Start the process by identifying and studying your sources of data: reviewing paper or electronic forms, combing the websites, reviewing current system documentation, consulting industry data standards, and of course interviewing the experts. Once you identify and record all the data and metadata, secure a tool that is specifically created to manage data (and maybe functional) requirements. There are a plethora of tools in the market that can assist you in effectively managing the requirements. But before you purchase a tool, make sure there isn't one available in your own backyard; check with your internal IT department, your business partners, and your clients to see what your options are before you make that purchase.

Follow the process that we outlined and discussed in this book to successfully complete the harmonization process and create a harmonized data set. Keep in mind that the process is iterative, and you may have to repeat it several times before you create a succinct accurate listing of data requirements. That's okay! Iterate as many times as needed to compose a listing that is agreed upon by the client, is comprehensive, and really resonates with all the stakeholders.

Preparing for and presenting your findings to the client is an extremely important task. Do not take this task lightly! Preparation is the key to success when planning and executing an effective presentation. During the presentation, take copious notes and gather all the feedback that you can regarding the accuracy and completeness of the artifacts. Afterward, carefully review and analyze the comments, notes, and feedback and then apply the updates and corrections to the work products. Don't be surprised to find that you may need to go through another round of harmonizing based on the feedback. Review the final product with your client, if time permits.

After spending all that time, money, and effort to produce the data artifacts, don't let them become ornaments on your client's bookshelf. Instead, use these artifacts as starting points for the next phase of the development cycle. A comprehensive data listing can easily become the foundation for a business-process reengineering effort or the basis for constructing logical and physical data models and entity relationship diagrams (ERD). Data analysis can provide a starting point for functional requirements and use cases. The point is this: *use* the results of your analysis!

As you move forward in the development life cycle, you'll revisit the data artifacts many more times. As updates occur, remember to consult the existing data standards for the industry you're working in and make an effort to align your business and data requirements to the framework of the industry's governing body or bodies. Keep in mind that you want to control the changes to the artifacts through an effective change control strategy and a rigorous data governance program. By doing so, you will reduce the amount of effort in the later stages of the life cycle, especially implementation.

I sincerely hope that you have enjoyed taking this journey into the world of data analysis and harmonization. I have certainly enjoyed being your tour guide! If and when you are faced with a task that is similar to the situations presented in these pages, I trust you will employ some or all of the techniques we've discussed to produce a set of great data artifacts that you can be proud of. Data is the most important corporate asset—manage it well!

GLOSSARY

accuracy: qualitative assessment of how well data reflects real-world objects or matches the original source of data

audit trail: documentation that records and stores any and all changes to a work product or artifact

authoritative data: officially recognized data that can be certified and is provided by an authoritative source

authoritative data source: a system process that assures the veracity of data sources (These processes should be followed by all providers of authoritative data.)

authoritative source: an entity that is authorized by a legal authority to develop, maintain or distribute specific data for a specific business purpose

Boolean element: a data element that may contain one of two values, either true or false

canned report: reports that the vendor has created and loaded into the software for use by the client

change management: a systematic method of administering, managing, and organizing reviews, updates, and implementation of work products and artifacts

CIO (chief information officer): This title generally refers to the most senior person in the enterprise responsible for the operations of the information technology that supports the organization's business goals.

COI (community of interest): a logical or physical grouping of data, devices, or users with access to specific information

completeness: the degree to which values are present in the attributes that require them

conceptual data model: an abstract model that represents the high-level view of an organization's concepts (functional areas) and the relationships between those concepts

consistency: the degree to which redundant facts are equivalent across two or more databases

contingent field: a data field that becomes active or is required when a related field is populated

COTS (commercial off-the-shelf): a software product that is available for purchase that serves a specific purpose for an organization

cross-boundary information exchange: an exchange of information that crosses a bureau or agency boundary, including information sharing with international, state, local, tribal, industry, or nongovernmental organization partners

data element: an atomic unit of data that has a precise meaning, usage, and business value to the entity that collects it

data governance: the creation and implementation of data standards that administer the collection, storage, and usage of data and metadata

data redundancy: a data anomaly that occurs when a data element is stored in more than one location or database simultaneously

data stewardship: the responsible management and maintenance of data and related metadata

DBA (database administrator): a person or persons responsible for design, implementation, and maintenance of an organization's data and databases

DDL (data definition language): any language that is used for describing and defining data and data structures

dependency: a scenario in which one data element is clarified or qualified by the existence of another related data element

enterprise architecture: a discipline that seeks to define the business organization (the enterprise) by decomposing the organization into its subsystems, defining the relationships between the subsystems, and identifying the data that is exchanged both within the enterprise and its subsystems and with the external actors

ERD (entity relationship diagram): a specialized graphic that illustrates entities, the attributes contained within the entities, and the interrelationships between those entities

harmonization: a set of actions or operations applied to a collection of raw, disparate data resulting in a consistent set of standard, agreed-upon, and comprehensive data elements that can be utilized and transmitted across and between the involved organizations

harmonized data set (HDS): a collection of data elements that represents a standardized, comprehensive, and agreed-upon set of data that accounts for all data requirements of an organization or entity

JAD (joint application development): a process used to collect business, functional, and system requirements as part of the life cycle of developing new information systems or reengineering current information systems for a company

line of business: a set of highly related products or services that provide data to stakeholders to fulfill their business data requirements

lineage: a mechanism for tracing where data originates, where it flows, and how it is transformed as it moves through the business process

logical data model: a method of representing an organization's data based on areas of interest, which are represented by objects called entities and the relationships between the entities (The logical model is more descriptive than the conceptual model.)

loner: a data element that is not harmonized; also referred to as an orphan

mandatory field: a data field that must be populated in order to complete the business process

metadata: the data that describes the data or information

MOA (memorandum of agreement): a document that describes the agreement between two entities that governs the cooperative actions to be taken by both parties in order to meet an agreed-upon objective

MOU (memorandum of understanding): a document that describes the agreement between two entities that identifies the intended set of actions to be taken by both parties

NIEM (National Information Exchange Model): a model designed to develop, disseminate, and support enterprise-wide information exchange standards and processes that can enable jurisdictions and organizations to effectively share information

normalization: a systematic method of ensuring that a database structure is suitable for general-purpose querying and free of data anomalies that could lead to a loss of data integrity and reliability

optional field: a data field that may be populated in order to complete the business process but is not considered mandatory

orphan: a data element that is not harmonized; also referred to as a loner

PDF (portable document format): a file format for information exchange that is independent of application software, hardware, and operating systems.

physical data model: This model represents a comprehensive database design including data fields, optionality, cardinality, as well as relationships and constraints between the entities. The physical data model usually is derived from the logical data model (but not always).

precision: the degree to which data is known to the right level of granularity

priority: an indicator, usually in the form of metadata, of the importance of the data element to the business

qualifier: a data element that clarifies or helps explain another related data element

relationship: a defined association between a specific data element and one or more other data elements

representation term: the word used to express the category of an individual data element

shredding: the process of analyzing, dissecting, and recording the individual data elements that comprise an entity's form

SME (subject matter expert): a person or other source of information that is generally considered the most knowledgeable of a specific subject area

sneakernet: a term used to describe the transfer of data and/or information by physical movement of the storage medium instead of electronic transfer of stored data

SOW (statement of work): the official document that captures and defines the activities, tasks, deliverables, milestones, and timelines that a vendor will adhere to in the execution of the work for the client

stovepipe system: a computer system whose functionality and processes are narrowly focused to provide specific data to a specific recipient

timeliness: the degree to which data is up-to-date and available to support a given knowledge worker or process

use case: a method of describing system behavior based on stimuli from an actor

uniqueness: the degree to which there are no redundant occurrences or records of the same object or event

validity: the degree to which data conforms to its definition, domain values, and business rules

XML (eXtensible Markup Language): a set of rules and provisions for encoding and facilitating electronic data interchange

REFERENCES

"ADS Data Quality Management," [2010] Citizant, Inc.

"American National Standards Institute," [2010] Available at: http://www.ansi.org/about_ansi/overview/overview. aspx?menuid=1\

Beynon-Davis, P. [2004]. *Database Systems,* (3rd ed.), Palgrave, Basingstoke, UK Available at: http://en.wikipedia.org/wiki/Data_ element

"Biodiversity Information Standards TDWG," [August 2007] Available at: http://www.tdwg.org/about-tdwg/

Chapple, Mike [2010]. *Entity-Relationship Diagram* About.com Guide Available at: http://databases.about.com/cs/specificproducts/g/ er.htm

Chavis, Jason C. [2003–2010]. *What is Metadata?* Conjecture Corporation Available at: http://www.wisegeek.com/what-is-metadata.htm

"Healthcare Information Technology Standards Panel," [2009]
Available at: http://www.hitsp.org/

"Information and Regulatory Affairs," [2010]
Available at: http://www.whitehouse.gov

"ISO International Organization for Standardization," [2010]
Available at: http://www.iso.org/iso/about.htm

"Leverage Your Data as an Enterprise Asset," [2009]
Available at: http://www.information-management.com

Marco, David [November 2009]. *Metadata Silos: Part 2* Enterprise
Information Management Institute.org
Available at: http://www.eiminstitute.org

Merriam-Webster Online [2010]. Merriam-Webster, Inc.
Available at: http://www.merriam-webster.com/dictionary

"National Information Exchange Model (NIEM) Practical
Implementer's Guide," [October 2009] IJIS Institute

"NIEM Bridging Information Systems," [2010]
Available at: http://www.niem.gov/

Sowell, P. K. [2007]. "Enterprise Architecture Certification
Program"
Available at: http://www.sowelleac.com

Stage, David [February 2009]. "Authority and Authoritative
Data: A Clarification of Terms and Concepts," *Fair and Equitable
Magazine*
Available at: http://www.iaao.org/uploads/Stage.pdf

"US FEA DRM (Federal Enterprise Architecture Data Reference Model)," [2008] Available at: http://www.datagovernance.com/fwo3_US_FEA_DRM.html

"World Customs Organization," [2010]
Available at: http://www.wcoomd.org/home_about_us.htm

www.ingramcontent.com/pod-product-compliance
Lightning Source LLC
Chambersburg PA
CBHW071203050326
40689CB00011B/2222